Smart First Touches

Developing the Skillful Player

Martin Bidzinski

Library of Congress Cataloging - in - Publication Data

Smart First Touches: Developing the Skillful Player
Bidzinski, Martin

ISBN No. 1-59164-078-4
Library of Congress Control Number 2004092403
© 2004

Art Direction, Layout, Cover Design, Diagrams and Editing
Bryan Beaver

Photographs
Richard Kentwell

Graphic Artist
Dan Spollen

Printed by
DATA REPRODUCTIONS
Auburn, Michigan

Reedswain Publishing
562 Ridge Road
Spring City, PA 19475
800.331.5191
www.reedswain.com
info@reedswain.com

CONTENTS

INTRODUCTION

What makes a great soccer player? Some would argue that speed and physical strength are the hallmarks of a good player, while others believe that skill is what sets a player apart. It is true that some of the more aggressive physical attributes can hide all sorts of deficiencies that are not at all obvious to the average fan and some managers do call upon physical play to deliver the so-called winning formula. However, if you believe in **'Coaching'** soccer players like I do, the approach to the players' development has to be different to that of any approach that is simply based on the physical side of the game. What I have tried to do is not to look at what the players' attributes should be in terms of anyone's opinion (Good, bad, or indifferent) but to look objectively at how to improve the players' (full) playing potential. I have come to the conclusion that it is in everyone's interest to work with the player in such a way that he/she should be able to compete at the highest levels, no matter what the style of play. My coaching system is specifically designed to cater to the **development of a player's talent** and has nothing at all to do with whether he is naturally gifted, right or left footed. I prefer instead to concentrate entirely on developing any player to be the best he can be (developing his potential) without accepting certain playing limitations.

THE PLAYING AND PRACTICE CONFLICT

There are events in the history of any country that can influence the way things are done in all walks of life. Once upon a time the game of soccer was a working man's game and reserved only for the boy or man who stood little chance of making it anywhere else. Women did not participate in sport and it was said that 'Football' was for men only. The game of soccer has, of course, changed beyond recognition, but the biggest strides made happened on the equipment side of the game. We have some of the finest stadiums in the world and players enjoy the use of better playing equipment such as soccer boots and kits, and of course the ball itself is no longer the dreaded head basher of the past. The least strides made as far as I am concerned have been in the area of **coaching players**. The game has moved on and now requires a professional approach to coaching. The development of players must be based on **understanding the playing environment**.

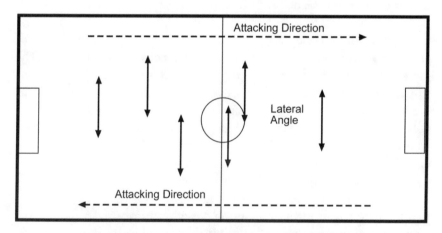

It may seem an obvious observation, but looking at the diagram above we see the possible playing directions in soccer (represented by the dotted lines). This is the way most coaches, players and fans view the game. The modern game is a vertical one. The play moves primarily up and down the field of play and thus most player movement is either straight ahead (attack) or straight back (recover). This view of the game can be attributed to Sir Alf Ramsey, who in 1966 coached England to a World Cup Championship by implementing the 4-3-1-2 which was then interpreted as the 4-3-3 system of play, in effect changing the expectations of what the attributes of any player should be. The premium was suddenly on big, strong aggressive players, and the coaching of skill and lateral movement has suffered ever since.

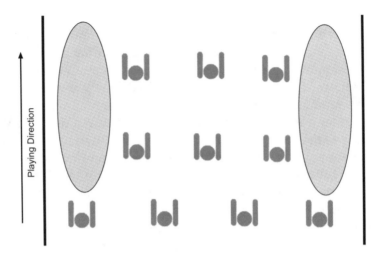

On The Practice Ground

It is simply not an accident that some of the more aggressive aspects of play were promoted to the detriment of the skills side of the game. The game of soccer is based on competition and, therefore, easy to manipulate. It is easy to isolate the aggressive elements and to bring those into the forefront of the working equation. The competitive battling attributes can be fostered in **small-sided games** and in tight areas of play where the player has very little time on the ball. Thanks to the player development programs that catered to aggressive play (and still do) there is an **alarming lack of skills** in home-grown (English) players today and certainly a lack of lateral training. It is logical to conclude that if a player is brought up in a one directional (forward movement) environment, not only his skills but his understanding of the wide range of playing options available to him will suffer.

Why should this be the case? The answer to that is simple: it is easy to miss the lateral development equation from the soccer training solutions when you cater to aggressive play. After all, the use of lateral movements (moving sideways) is not something that the human being does on a daily basis. Most human activities, such as walking, jogging, running and jumping, take place in a natural forward direction.

It is therefore not inconceivable that the majority of player movement in practice sessions (and subsequently in matches) takes place in a vertical direction.

When the lateral angle is not applied to the working equation there are serious consequences to the physical development of the player that I need to mention here. Many common soccer injuries (groin, knee, hamstring, etc.) are the direct result of a lack of lateral training, which obviously leads to a lack of lateral physical strength. Overuse or misuse of weight training has also contributed to decreased lateral development and injury. While it is true that weight training is essential in specialized areas of development such as the upper body, when a player works with weights incorrectly the effects of training can be devastating. The wrongful development of the player's hamstring, for example, in relation to his running stride contributes to a higher than average injury incidence to this important area of the body. The sad fact of life today is that there are people out there who are hungry for success and who as a result of that hunger rush into the weight training room far too early in life and fail to recognize the need for caution. The correct development of the player should be based on the working principle that -

'The weight of the body and the consequences of gravity form a specific working environment - this environment can only be overcome through the application of physical power - that power comes from the contraction of the muscles to produce physical effort and when that physical effort exceeds the resistance of gravity, motion takes place.'

In simple terms, therefore, the development of the player needs to adhere to the basic training philosophy that - **'MUSCLES REACT TO EFFORT AND DEVELOP ACCORDINGLY'**

What does that mean in terms of 'Soccer Training'

I believe that it is important to develop the player in such a way that he/she will possess a greater range of physical movements. The key to developing different technical and physical attributes, therefore, lies in working in a physical environment that is directly related to the job of playing soccer. Since lateral angles and resistance forms of training produce the best physical and technical development results, most formats need to take this into consideration. It is important to utilize the correct methods of training to achieve the correct development objectives.

Understanding Different Forms Of Training

Today's game requirements must be based on a coaching technique that caters to the development of a different type of player, a player with a much greater range of playing options. Therefore, it is important to understand different forms of training and the effects of them on the development of the player.

For Example

Some people believe that if a player pulls something heavy behind him, he will develop his strength for running. Of course, it is possible to gain something from this exercise, but when it comes to running objectives for soccer, things are far more complicated, and pulling a heavy object would only cover a fraction of the player's needs. Why is that? The number one reason is that it does not address **proper running technique.** The solution lies in implementing a wide range of training options that  take both the technique of running and the physical resistance associated with running into consideration. It is possible to target any number of physical problems associated with running and coaches should look to do that rather than limit the player to any set physical working pattern. **Sometimes the simplest exercises can give you the greatest results.** Take a practical look at the circle exercise on page 54, in which the player develops the correct running attributes because the movements within the circle adhere not only to the principles of developing the stride for running but also the strength for running. I will explain why later in the book.

The following work adheres to a **well-balanced and varied player development program.** A program that covers a far greater range of concerns in respect to the players' needs than any conventional method of training could ever achieve. Don't get me wrong, conventional methods of training go hand in hand with this training concept.

However, unlike other aggressive forms of training the following formats target directly the development of the physical and technical skills for soccer because the skills of soccer are defined by the working formats. It is my belief that the quality of the development of different playing attributes cannot be left to any one directional training format, be it a soccer drill or a 'one footed' training environment. This is because most soccer training exercises do not define the skills of soccer in practical terms to any good effect.

It is not always accepted that the natural instincts of human beings can be worked on and improved with training. The truth is that no matter how naturally talented a player is, it is still essential to work on and develop that player if he is to reach his full potential. There is a saying that 'Practice makes Perfect' and that is of course true to some extent. Everyone knows that prolonged activities that keep to the same working sequence will always have an effect on the development of the player but all too often this fact has contributed to the wrongful understanding of player development guidelines. In soccer, whether a player is right or left footed should not be the guideline on how to develop his full playing potential.

The Development of Good & Bad Habits

At first hand some human traits may or may not be conceived as relevant to the development of different soccer skills. However, people (in general terms) like to make things as easy as possible and this can influence matters on the training ground and indeed on the soccer pitch as well. We all need to recognize that there are good and bad working habits in any endeavor. In soccer it is no different. Most players do develop good and bad working habits, depending on the way they have been trained. You may be surprised just how many players out there today find solutions based on a rigid set of rules laid out by the coach. If you agree that this is often the case then you should also realize straight away that the outcome of any coaching system determines how a player plays the game. Clearly, if the training system is incorrect then the effects on the player will be damaging. High standards of play are determined by the **elimination of mistakes**.

The Acquisition of Strength & Good Playing Habits

Some forms of natural human behavior will be very helpful to the player's development program and some will not be so helpful. I will use the best habitual behavior instincts of the player to develop his full potential. What does this mean in terms of training? Remember that players are people and there are any number of reasons that can get in the way of progress. Players can be:

(a) **averse to change**: "Oh no! The ball is on my left foot! I can't play the ball!" or
(b) **willing to change**: "No problem, I can play the ball!"

It is therefore important to start working with the player correctly from an early age and to foster an open mind to training. The approach to the player's development problems must always air on the positive side of the player's attitude and thinking process. It is impossible to develop high standards of play by ignoring the obvious in the above example. If the above negative and limited side of the working equation (a) is an option readily available to the player, he will not improve his playing attributes to his full potential. A good training session will always foster the positive approach to playing the ball (b) with the correct foot where required to do so.

It must be obvious to everyone by now that when the ball comes to a player on his left side, he should be able to play the ball with the left foot. If the player is allowed to get into the habit of adjusting his body position to accommodate his strong foot in any playing situation, he will not develop to his full potential. The inability to play the ball with the weak foot at any point in time is a fault that causes a reduction in the player's options. For example, in badly developed players it is common that right-footed players play the game primarily on the right side of the pitch. There are lots of different reasons for this, but the most common of all reasons has to be that the right-footed player cannot play the ball easily to his left when closed down (challenged) by an opponent. It is amazing just how many people don't realize this simple yet important point.

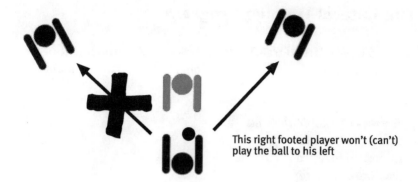

This right footed player won't (can't) play the ball to his left

My contention has always been that the ability to play the ball to the right or left should not be a problem or a controversial issue. The habit to do so should be instilled in every player from a very early age. Remember that ignorance of such playing limitations sets the future playing standards of the game. There are far too many players out there today who are physically underdeveloped and rely entirely on their "one good foot" to play soccer. The lack of commitment to address this problem allows the player to take the easy option of moving the ball to the right of his position and to simply settle for being one footed. It is a sad thing that this issue is not addressed properly and far too many people out there still believe that it does not matter. I believe that it is in the interest of the game and the future of the players themselves that these attitudes towards a one-footed player change and more coaches and players make a **commitment to making their "weaker foot" a viable playing option**.

Apply The Following Training Concepts

The following lateral development program endeavors to change things and to work on and develop both the right and left side of the player. The working formats, right up to the 'Match Play' circuits, cover the needs of the player in every respect save one, namely the playing of the game of soccer, which of course takes place in the actual games.

The Lateral Training Program

In the following lateral training environment the development of the player centers on his ability to move physically with and without the ball in the following areas;

Defensive - Physical Movements
- Lateral to backward
- Lateral to forward
- Backwards to lateral
- Backwards to lateral to forward
- Backwards to lateral to forward to lateral to backwards
- Special jockeying 'Angled' movements backwards/right/left

Offensive - Physical Movements
- Forward direction
- Angled forward right/left
- Lateral (fast feet)
- Economical movements
- Change in pace
- Fast Feet /Pace
- Physical Agility
- Physical - Playing 'off' 'The first touch'

The Major Working Principle - The physical development of the player must be balanced in terms of his strength and technical attributes. By balanced I mean that the player's ability to move with and without the ball to any direction is a prime consideration where the development of the player will focus on a wide range of training objectives. It is essential to create a training environment that will enable the player to work on and develop both the right and left side of the body. It is absurd to say that the weak side of the body cannot be developed to a level of competence that is in line with the best playing expectations. **If the training is appropriate the player can develop the necessary mechanics to play soccer without limitations.**

It is impossible for a player to develop balanced movement capabilities (physical strength on both the right and left side of the body) without the use of lateral forms of training. There are serious reasons why only the lateral forms of training can deliver the practical strength required to use both feet and to perform many of soccer's physical objectives. Different playing solutions can only be implemented or performed on the pitch if the player is developed physically in a balanced way and therefore strong on both the right and left side of the body. In terms of the correct player development programs, it should be the case that all formats should endeavor to deliver the **physically balanced player**.

Include The Upper Body

The training of the player should center on two physical areas of concern, namely the upper and lower part of the body. Everyone should keep in mind that because the bulk of the effort put forth by a soccer player in a match comes from the lower part of the body, the upper body will not work as hard during play. This has to be taken into account and the upper part of the body will need additional attention.

Leading To A Lack Of Proportionality?

It is not a good idea to leave the shoulders and arms untrained for any length of time because with time it will mean a marked physical imbalance between the upper and lower parts of the body. The upper body will not balance out physically with the lower body in terms of stature or the strength required for playing soccer. If one part of the body is bulky and strong and another is weak and thin, problems in terms of the player's ability to move correctly with or without the ball can occur. More importantly, some physical instability can lead to injuries. The proportionally built player will stand a better chance of playing at a higher level and his risk of injury will be minimized.

Note: I believe that up to the age of fourteen every player should be allowed to develop his body naturally. By this I mean utilizing the development concepts of the lateral training environment as opposed to weight training. Children grow very quickly and for that reason it is vital to work with exercises that mirror the game of soccer. In my experience the best way to develop the overall strength of any young player during the early stages is to apply the lateral formats and to use as many natural exercises as possible. Simple forms of training such as catching the ball, sit ups, push-ups or lifts will do. Prior to each training session, for example, every young player should spend a little time during the warm up doing simple upper body exercises with a ball such as a throw and catch at two yards apart.

This may seem a rather feeble attempt at developing the upper body for younger players and yet it is surprising just how much progress young players will make. In terms of upper and lower body development, it is definitely not a good idea to use weight training to build strength at too early an age. For young players, weight training is not the solution. The secret to upper body development lies in taking your time and working naturally with the player's own body weight.

Note: With sit ups, don't allow the player to do short body movements, work on the full sit up action. When a player works on his muscle and tendon development for playing 'Soccer' he needs to work on developing the muscles and tendons in a way that ensures the greatest freedom and range of movement.

From fifteen years of age -
Of course it is vital to look to develop the whole body by utilizing the weight training room for certain physical development solutions for older players (from fifteen years of age). It is possible to introduce the player to lightweight fast movement repetition work for the upper body as a supplement to the overall training program. However, keep in mind that the choreography message in this respect is very different than the conventional message on weight training. Special weight training for the upper part of the body is fine for older age groups because that's the part of the body that needs additional attention due to the nature of playing soccer. However, the message in respect to the development of the player's overall physical balance, especially in the legs, is different to that of any conventional message no matter what age you are working with. I believe that the lateral training program based on **kinetic tension** makes it unnecessary for the player to work extensively in the weight training room on the legs. This contention is misunderstood for different reasons. **I do not subscribe to the view that a player needs to be ready to play professionally at age fifteen.** Often the rush to do so encourages many a young player into the weight training room far too early with sad consequences, especially if he ends up being developed incorrectly in terms of agility or skill. It is essential to keep an eye on the overall physical shape of the player and not to overdo things in any one area. Any player who adds unnatural muscle mass early on through weight training has a good chance of achieving less mobility than a player who is proportionally built and well balanced. **Being less mobile does amount, in most cases, to being less skilful**.

GROWTH SPURTS

There will always be problems associated with growth spurts at different stages of a player's physical development that you can't do anything about. Also, some of the technical development aspects of play cannot possibly come to the forefront early on because of the player's physical limitations. Some soccer skills require a physically mature player. For example, look at the length of the physical movements that move the foot over the ball in a sweep action. Young players will not be able to move the ball effectively simply because their legs are too short. The lateral training concept considers the natural growth of the player and therefore targets the development of the player's physical needs and his mental skills as well throughout his physical development. It is important to be patient with the results and to keep in mind that the characteristics of any individual player will eventually come through to make that player into a striker or a midfield player or a defender. Not everyone will possess the imagination or the talent to reach the standards required at the top of the profession. Ultimately, a player's progress will always depend on his own:

(a) **Dedication** - The development of the player depends on his effort.
(b) **Practice** - Learning to practice rather than play and appreciating the need to work on the technical aspects of the game ensures success.

LATERAL DEVELOPMENT

The First Rule Of Development

Every player should be **comfortable with the ball** and be able to move the ball against the defender, **to the right or left** at will. The need for physical strength on both the right and left side of the body is clear. If the player is strong but only on one side of the body, as is often the case, then I can assure you that the right footed player's discomfort in moving to his left will put a happy face on the defender. It is a fact that the development of a player's ability to move the ball to the right or left of the defender raises standards of play. It is not a question of leaving things to nature, you need to apply **specialized forms of training** to achieve certain physical capabilities.

Consider this - The highest standards of play require top class players. Top clubs cannot stay at the top of their respective league if the players on their books have playing limitations. In today's game, the playing attributes far outstrip yesterday's requirements. The attacking player at the highest levels of the game must be able to move the ball to any direction and the defender should not be able to dictate his playing options.

THE TRAINING SOLUTIONS

Obviously, the ability to play the ball to any direction cannot be achieved in a training format based solely on forward movement with the ball. Since most human beings are born with a dominant 'Physical & Mental' side of the body, one side of the player's body will naturally be the weaker side. When the weak side is left out of the training equation, it will become more and more underdeveloped and less able to adapt to any playing situation. The lack of proper training guidelines and objectives will cause the player to be physically unbalanced and one footed, leaving him with limited playing options.

The Essential Lateral Training Format

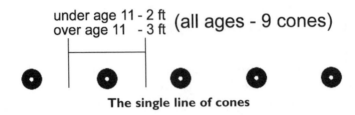

under age 11 - 2 ft
over age 11 - 3 ft (all ages - 9 cones)

The single line of cones

The first solution is to develop the player's **physical strength** on both the right and left side of the body. Once the player develops the ability to move the ball with the right inside instep and the left inside instep, he will possess the ability to move the ball to the left or to the right of his playing position. The above line of cones is utilized for working on this crucial early physical development objective. From a physical 'lateral development' point of view (when working on the physical strength on both the right and left side of the body) the above format can be said to be the basis for all other working formats. I will explain the above format in terms of the chronology relationship (the skills development link) to other essential skills of soccer in the following chapter. It is sufficient for now to say that the above line of cones is probably the most deceptive of any of my working exercises. You will find that this simple line of cones enables the player to work on the most essential foundational abilities of all the physical and technical requirements that he will need as a player. The work undertaken is essential to the development of the ability to hold a **'square on'** body position.

The Training Effects - The training effects of the above format lay the foundations for the correct physical development of the player's strength on both the left and right side of his body. The most important function of the above format is as follows -

1. The development of the player's ability to stay 'Square on'
2. The development of the player's strength (groin)
3. The development of lateral movements /skills

The Development Objectives - The first task set for the player is to work the ball down the line of cones by using the **inside instep**. The player practices moving the ball from gap to gap and from one inside instep to the next. The ability to play with a square on body position (lateral to the action) comes from developing strength in the inner groin. It is the action performed by the player parallel to the line of cones that develops some of the most essential player attributes. The actual length of touch at this stage should equal the player's shoulder width. The inside instep sideways action develops the balanced physical strength the player needs to move the ball when performing different play options.

Right instep moves the ball ➝ Left instep stops the ball

By moving the ball with the inside instep from one gap to the next in a rhythmic manner, the player secures the correct development of the groin and the inner muscle groups of the legs and body. The kinetic tension from the amount of times the player moves the ball with the inside instep down the line of cones creates a better density in the bone structure of the lower body and therefore a stronger physical capability. The above illustration represents the sideways movement involved in passing the ball between the inside instep of the right foot and the inside instep of the left foot. This will achieve the following results:

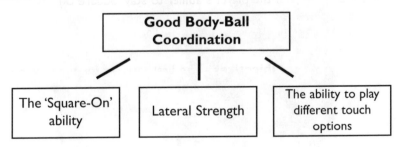

The following explanation shows how easy it is to achieve and maintain physical balance. Just follow this simple rule: If the player begins his work on the right side of the line of cones, he should repeat the working sequence from the left after a set number of starts.

The working principles - It is always prudent to make sure that the player works the ball to the right and left direction in the line of cones format in equal amounts to maintain physical balance. The single line of cones format lays down the physical and technical foundations for the development of the player's strength on both the left and right side of the body. In turn, the development of the strength on both sides of the body (the ability to play the ball to the lateral angle with both feet) will give the player the potential to play various skill options. The playing options are best explained by looking at the effects of the different formats in the following chronological relationship. In practical terms the simple inside instep work practiced in the above straight line of cones format develops the necessary skill base for 'one on one' skill solutions. The relationship between the 'straight line of cones' and other formats (different soccer skills) is shown by the following working table.

Laying Down 'The Foundations'

The development of playing skills goes hand in hand with physical development. The most important skill to learn at the outset is the simple inside instep to inside instep move to the lateral angle. The secret of skill development lies in the mastering of this simple movement with the ball. Once this is achieved the player can begin to develop a whole range of skills. The diagram on the next page shows how a single line of cones gives birth to other working formats.

The Progressive Link

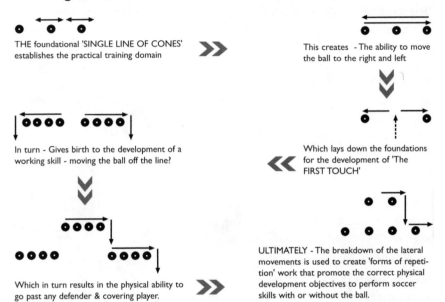

THE foundational 'SINGLE LINE OF CONES' establishes the practical training domain

This creates - The ability to move the ball to the right and left

In turn - Gives birth to the development of a working skill - moving the ball off the line?

Which lays down the foundations for the development of 'The FIRST TOUCH'

Which in turn results in the physical ability to go past any defender & covering player.

ULTIMATELY - The breakdown of the lateral movements is used to create 'forms of repetition' work that promote the correct physical development objectives to perform soccer skills with or without the ball.

The single lateral (straight) line of cones is indeed essential to the development of different lateral soccer skills. Once the player has mastered the simple inside instep lateral (sideways) movements with the ball he will be in a position to move into the different lateral training exercises on offer. The above table shows the progressive stages of the different elements. There are countless benefits to the lateral method of training, the first being that they are quite easy for any player to learn or recognize. The shapes of the formats dictate the purpose of their function on the practice ground and players will quickly be able to associate each shape with the skill involved. It should be clear at this stage that the shapes represent the physical composition of a soccer skill. Once the player knows what to do in any given shape, he will be in a good position to perform a particular skill.

The Simple Translation

Appreciating the reasons for the need to develop different skills is of course essential to the understanding of the working formats. Whether a player is naturally talented or not, high standards of play will always depend on the player's ability to apply any soccer skill correctly. The ability to do so depends on knowing what the game is about and what skills to apply in a given situation. What you see on the soccer pitch in the following examples will (surprisingly for many players) not always be obvious or indeed physically possible to achieve for many of them because they will not be in possession of the skills or the knowledge to do so.

Reading The Game

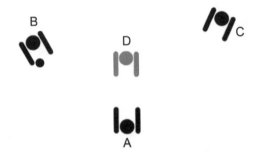

During Play - The assessment by player B of his playing options has to be done very quickly - Does he, for example, play the ball to player A in a way that considers the position of the defender? What should happen when player A receives the ball? Should the pass favor player A's right or left foot? On the other hand, does player B play the ball in front of player A or behind him, taking into account the defender's position? Of course the player on the ball should consider such issues but to do so is not easy. In the majority of cases players who are taught incorrectly because of a lack of lateral formats in practice cannot consider all the above playing options in equal terms. Most play the game in a surprisingly improvised manner with playing attributes that either enhance or reduce their capability.

WHAT ARE THE PLAYING OPTIONS?

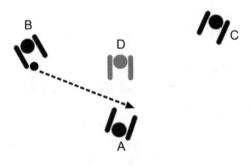

In this simple example of how to **read the game**, the pass should be made to player A's right foot. Playing the pass to his right foot would enable him to open up his playing options. It would be wrong to play the ball to player A's left foot because that pass would give the defender (D) time to reduce the attacking options. A positive outcome is dependant on both player B and player A. This is a simple example of why it is vital that every player has the ability to play the ball with both feet. Even in the most simple playing scenarios, there are lots of skills that need to come into play to make the play work. It is worth repeating that the actual choice of action results from the player's playing capabilities. If those are limited, then the choice of what to do with the ball will also be limited. If the defender knows that the receiving player cannot play the ball with his right foot, the choice of action would also be limited by the defender's ability to influence the game. It is logical, therefore, to assume that it is the player's ability to read the game and to implement the appropriate playing solutions that makes all the difference to the outcome. **Negative results come from a lack of playing ability.** The best way to develop higher standards of play is to develop good habits. You may be surprised to know that it is not too difficult to teach the players good habits that will become instinctive on the pitch. The ability to read the game is a question of how the body works in relation to different playing options and how to apply the different playing options to the questions asked on the pitch. The whole secret to the player's development, therefore, is based on developing his body movements in relation to the ball and his playing options.

Move on the touch

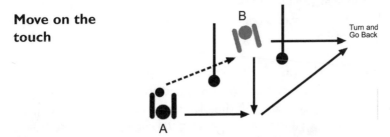

B

Turn and Go Back

A

Turn and go back
Pass & Move - The practice task set in any format (the above example is as simple as it gets) should be based on a practical playing requirement. All of the formats set out here are designed to create the correct working physical and technical effect for the acquisition of the different soccer playing skills. The correct playing habits, therefore, are based on the specific physical movements required to solve the playing solutions.

A Working Example -Above is a simple method of working on economical movements around two sticks. Two players play one-twos between the sticks then turn and go back. Body shape and correct touch are essential elements to the success of this format. The wrong body position can cause the foot to impart spin on the ball which in turn will cause the receiver of the ball problems on his pass/touch. Experiencing problems of this nature and working to a specific movement pattern cuts out wasting time on explanations and affords the player a working environment that enables him to work on and develop the necessary skills to play the ball both from a physical and technical point of view. For example, when it comes to the bio-mechanical side of the working equation, the player learns how and when to play the ball with the inside instep or when to play the ball with the laces part of the boot. Playing the ball around the sticks involves developing the ability to play the ball off the first touch and to move off that touch to either receive the ball or to pass the ball back. The pass and move sequence (past the sticks) in the above format includes the use of a body turn.

Note - The learning process is based on the unfortunate fact of life that all players make mistakes initially when they are given a set task to perform. The most common mistake that all players make is not applying the correct amount of follow through on the touch/pass of the ball. The working formats are designed in a way that results in a learning process that helps the player to spot mistakes and to correct them quickly. In the above format the players will soon learn that a lack of follow through influences what happens to the ball/pass in terms of accuracy and keeping the practice going fluently.

Practical Experience
The best way to learn comes from the need to make any format work to the rules set by the coach. If the players move incorrectly, the practice will break down. In the above format the movements, together with the starting position of the players and the direction of the work, creates the proper working conditions for development of the ability to play the 'one-two'. In terms of player development the simplicity of the movements is not in question here, what matters is the way the players move and pass the ball. When the players do things correctly, the transfer value of the practice is worth every kick of the ball. Of course, the key to the player's development is the practice of a wide

variety of 'Soccer skill movements'. With these working formats the development of the player takes place automatically in a way that fosters good playing habits, providing that the player pays attention to the details of the movements and carries those out to the letter. This may sound like a tall order but it is very natural for a player to learn a movement pattern sequence and to perform that sequence of movements consistently.

Note - In the sticks - Down & Back - When the player arrives at the far end of the sticks after completing the one-two pass and move sequence, he has to think about where to pass the ball next and whether the pass should be made to feet or to space. Both players have to think constantly during the sequence. In the above example, the sequence starts with pass option 1. This pass is made to space in front of player B who starts his work on the other side of the two sticks. Pass option 2 is made by player B, again in front of the runner (into space) A. Pass option 3 is made to the left foot (to feet) of the now turning player B, again on the other side of the stick. Pass option 4 will be played back to player A who is turning and so on. None of the skills in question should take place without both players having the ability to play with their heads up on the move and play the ball with the right and left foot. Looking up should take place 'off the first touch' or before a pass is made.

The working balance - It is in the interest of the players to change roles or swap places after a short working sequence in order to promote balanced development.

Passing the ball - There is a simple way to explain the use of the foot position and the body position during the pass. If the body -

Is in an upright position = Use The 'Inside instep'
Leans to the side = Use 'The Laces' part of the foot

Note - For body position options when passing, see 'The Figure Eight' example.

THE DIFFERENCE IN PLAYING SKILLS

It is virtually impossible to learn the skills of soccer properly during actual play, especially when an opponent is battling to win possession of the ball and the player in possession of the ball has very little room to play. Most players when in possession in tight spaces will improvise a great deal to get out of trouble. This is the major reason why I believe that in developing the actual skills of soccer it is essential to first and foremost define the skills of soccer for the player and then to bring those definitions into a practical training environment. The application of the working formats involves understanding the difference between the various skills of soccer - for example -

What Is a Close Ball Control Skill?

In this first example, we have the defender challenging the player in possession of the ball. When the defender puts pressure on the attacker, the latter will have no option but to lower his head (look down) and look at the ball. That's a good defensive position for the defender but what about the attacking player? The head down position of the attacking player will obviously reduce his vision and therefore his playing options. Moreover, he will not be able to see the position of other opponents or his own teammates. The only course of action left is to use a 'close ball control skill' to get himself out of trouble. In this example, the attacker has used the under-  side of the boot (his left boot) to drag (flick) the ball back under his body and turn away from the defender. A close ball control skill is, therefore, a skill that keeps the ball close to the body but away from the opponent's reach.

What Are Dribbling Skills?

The skill of dribbling with the ball has been somewhat misinterpreted by conventional thinking and most people think of dribbling skills and close ball control skills as being one and the same thing. Close ball control skills like the above example have a different function to that of the dribbling skills. By definition - Close ball control skills are 'used to keep the ball close to the body in tight areas of play. Dribbling skills, on the other hand, are different because they are used to go past opponents when the opponent has not yet achieved a controlled (head down on the ball) defensive position. The difference in terms of the choreography of the two skills in question (dribbling and close ball control skills) can be described by the following example.

THE ART OF DRIBBLING

The practical definition of the skills in use is as follows - *Arrow action 1*- Attacker moves the ball forward with the inside instep of the left foot. *Arrow action 2* - Attacker moves the ball off the line to the lateral angle (to the side of the defender) The touch that moves the ball to the side is made with the underside of the left boot. *Arrow action 3* -Attacker takes another forward touch to the ball (short) past the defender. When it comes to moving the ball past the defender (touches 2 and 3) the lateral to forward sequence of touches are combined effectively to create 'The side to forward' skill combination. See the 'Inverted Steps' format for this combination. The all-important point about the dribbling skills shown here is that these involve taking a specific touch to the ball. All standard skill options have a specific working pattern and, therefore, physical shape. The skill of 'Moving the ball off the line' is performed to an average touch distance of around 1.5 yards and there are four basic foot positions when working the ball off the line (See the chapter on first touch options). There are slow skill options and fast skill options. Arguably, one of the quickest of all physical movements on the ball involves the use of the underside of the boot to the ball (sweep).

The application of skills - In general, a skill can be implemented when the player is in motion or practically standing still. The lack of motion when in possession of the ball can cause the player problems because it is more difficult to work the ball from a static position. It is simply easier to work the ball on the move. Receiving the ball also has its implications. The pace on the pass can make all the difference to the first receiving touch and therefore the success of the play depends not only on the skill of the receiver but on the skill of the passer to recognize the type of pass that will be most effective.

When Receiving 'The Ball' - The four receiving options are simple to define. If the ball has the correct pace the player can take up the ball with the inside instep and move to the desired direction with the same foot. The difference between the four ways of working the ball lies in the way the foot is used. One way is shown by the above sweep action that moves the ball across the player's body. The other option is taking the same foot to the ball but playing it away from the body by extending the foot in the direction of the touch.
2 feet x 2 options = 4 options.

Note - Whether the player sweeps the ball or extends the foot on the touch to the direction of the touch, it is vital that the foot in contact with the ball moves off to the direction of the touch.

The Need To Know

I have described to you the basic touch options needed to create the lateral training environment. Once we know the basic touches and the basic formats we can construct a simple lateral format that will enable the player to begin to work on and develop any number of skills. The translation of all the above information into practical formats is as follows -

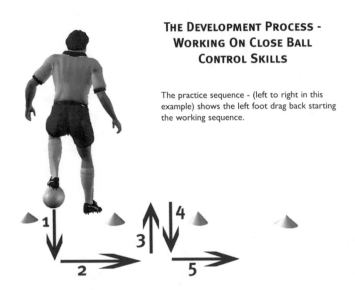

THE DEVELOPMENT PROCESS - WORKING ON CLOSE BALL CONTROL SKILLS

The practice sequence - (left to right in this example) shows the left foot drag back starting the working sequence.

The Development Strategy

The development strategy is therefore simple to define. The practice considerations take into account the differences in the playing scenarios. We know that there are going to be different ways that player A will have to use the ball and his body during play. The playing effects therefore require the development of different ways of handling the ball. The first example concentrates on the development of the player's overall foundational abilities.

The following skills can be worked on:

Position 1 - The left underside of the boot drags the ball back.
Position 2 - The lateral touch with the same foot (inside instep)
Positions 3 & 4 - The forward (short length of touch) punch through with the inside instep of the right foot, this touch moves the ball through the gap in the line of cones. The working sequence continues without a pause and the Left foot drags the ball back (using the underside of the left boot on top of the ball).

28

Note - When the player works the ball from his left to right, it is the left foot that drags the ball back and the right foot that punches the ball through the gap to the other side of the line of cones. When working the ball 'right to left' it is the right foot that drags the ball back and the left foot that punches the ball through the gap. In the above example, the lateral arrows indicate the use of the inside instep of the left foot to move the ball to the side.

The Working Sequence - In the single line of cones example, the theme of the practice is centered on the left inside instep and the underside of the left boot. To keep the ball moving through the format the action of the left foot is supported by the right foot, punching the ball through the line (see arrow 3 for example). Arrow 3 represents the short forward punch through of the ball and arrow 4 represents the drag back to ensure the continuation of the sequence. In keeping to the physical and technical balance agenda - Make sure that the player works the ball down the line of cones from right to left and vice versa on equal terms and that he works the ball to the same sequence.

Rhythm & Style
Developing different skills -The development of different skills of soccer should be based on a rhythmic style of practice wherever possible. One of the more important reasons for doing so is based on the little known fact that rhythmic movements on the ball produce a better bone density. Other benefits include an improvement in the player's ball control capability. In the previous example the rhythmic factor comes from keeping to the set (can be changed if required) working pattern across and down the line of cones, without pausing. The momentum of the movements involved also has the effect of improving the player's stamina and therefore ability to move his feet faster when dealing with the ball. Fast feet help the player to keep the ball and of course to implement his playing solutions.

The Formation Of Playing Combinations - The work in the single line of cones may look simple but it is the necessary first step in developing the player's understanding of the physical ability to combine two or more skills. When playing the ball against a second defender, for example, the player would have to shorten the length of touch and the feet would have to work a great deal faster. All formats are related and the work in the single line of cones leads to the players' understanding of what skills to use and when. In the above example, the resulting combination sequence could involve the drag back with the underside of the boot, the inside instep sideways touch and the forward touch options. It is easy to see the relationship between the work done in the straight line of cones and the skills on offer.

From A Playing Perspective

The best way to learn the value of any playing skill is of course to apply the skills in the actual game of soccer. Given time the player soon learns where and when to apply the skills in question. In practical terms, close ball control skills, like the 'Drag back' for example, are used in the following playing scenarios-

(a) Under pressure - When there is very little time or room to play.
(b) When the player is in a static playing position (caught in possession)
(c) When the player has his head down in possession
(d) When the player is restricted in his playing directions and options of play.

Moving the ball off the line is performed when -

(a) There is plenty of time and space on the ball
(b) When the player needs to change the pace of his work dramatically
(c) When the player wants to open up other playing possibilities
(d) When the player wants to change his playing direction
(e) When the player is moving past/away from the challenging player

The Development Of 'The First Touch'

The development of the first touch is a completely different issue. The first touch can only be played properly when the player has learned the specific movement requirements and therefore his body position in relation to a specific first touch option. Since there are in fact various first touch options that are foundational to the game of soccer (without which no one can play the game to any great effect) we need to go through some of the issues here. Most of the foundational first touch options are played from a 'Square on' body position, some are played when the player has his back to the opponent's goal and some start from a sideways on body position. In terms of the quality of the game and therefore touches on the ball there is a need to pay attention to the technical details of developing the first touch for lots of good reasons. The main points of reference again being the difference between the skills in question and their function on the soccer pitch. In this system of training the first touch is defined by a specific name and this is then supported by a practical training format that allows the player to work on the first touch.

THE FOUR CONE PLACEMENT

2 yds

2 yds

1 yd

THE FIRST TOUCH OPTIONS

The first touch options and related formats are used to enable the player not only to learn how to handle the ball but also to learn how to play with vision and use the playing space around him on the pitch.

1 - The Forward Touch

To further the explanation of the working formats I have chosen 'The Four - Cone Placement' format to introduce the 'The forward touch' example. The 'Four Cone Placement' at this juncture has nothing at all to do with the actual explanation of how to develop the first touch. Instead the introduction of the 'The Forward Touch' here and now is done in order to continue to take a look at the skills needed to construct a practical lateral training format. (If you want to know how to develop the first touch see the chapter on first touch options) In simple terms, what I have done up to this point in time is look at some of the foundational skills of soccer that are essential to the development of the player. 'The forward touch' completes the skill requirement for the creation of not only the understanding of what is involved in some working formats but also what it takes to construct a practical working format.

Note - The General Strategy - As far as the overall development of the player is concerned all concepts should present the player with the chance to work on and develop his touch in different playing circumstances. The construction of the working formats should be game related. If the formats represent fragments from the game it is not inconceivable that every player will be able to cover all playing eventualities sooner or later, providing of course that you employ a wide range of training considerations. To be fair to the reader it is vital to explain the forward touch at this point because it is this touch that is foundational to most playing solutions. The forward touch links up the use of different skills and therefore enables the player to develop the movements related to his playing solutions. It is also worth noting that first touch options can give the player the chance to look up and assess his playing situation.

In order to help you understand the working of the playing sequence I should say that the 'forward touch' is played from a 'Square On' upright body position (facing the ball) and the ball is picked up using the inside instep. The ball is played to the front of the player. The length of the forward touch is again about 1.5 yards on average.

Note - *The range of first touch options* - There are several important first touch options available to the player. The most important of them have names like 'The set up touch'. This touch is represented by the number 1 in the appropriate chapter on the development of the first touch. 'Moving the ball off the line' is represented by the number 2 - and 'The 'Forward Touch' is presented by number 3. In different playing scenarios the playing of the first touch i.e. 'The Forward Touch' is applied to solve different playing problems and the chapter on the first touch will make that clearer.

In practical terms, it is possible to combine the working elements (skills) in a way that would always give the player the correct working sequence that would simulate a realistic playing solution. I have based all working formats and their practice function on the actual game of soccer. These are in fact translations of the actual game. That being the case, you need only learn the shapes of the resulting cone placements. When you know the outline of the cone placements you will learn to recognize the relevant playing scenarios and the skills involved. It is that simple. In other words, the following working formats will give up their secrets to you once you position the cones on the practice ground and practice the movements. All practice formats (shapes) here are designed to reflect on all the major playing requirements of the game. Keep in mind that the training method is also reflective of the need to work in a way that considers several important principles of training - without which no one could possibly play effective soccer. The built in considerations are -

1 - The Development of the Strength to Play Soccer
2 - The Development of the Technique to Play Soccer
3 - The Acquisition of a Playing Repertoire

It is the practice of the movements and the use of the ball in conjunction with those movements that develops a player's ability to play soccer. One of the main differences when you apply the working formats into the practice equation comes from the fact that the player has the opportunity to work with the ball. The ball together with the task in hand creates the proper working conditions for the development of the player's lateral strength. Therefore, the development of the technique is also achieved by working the ball appropriately through any format. The setup can be very simple or complex depending on what the make up of the format entails. In the following example, the working theme is focused on the development of the lateral abilities (keeping the ball away from the oncoming challenger) together with the ability to keep the ball when caught in possession. The first format is made up of three separate sections - First, the single line of cones that you already know about which forms the close ball control component. If you then take a look on the left side you will see that we have an additional shape which deals with the skill of moving the ball 'off the line' against the first and second defender. If you feel that the overall shape is too complicated to begin with then simply work on taking on one defender, this is shown on the right hand side of the format.

THE COMBINED WORKING FORMAT

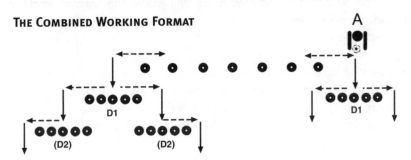

33

The working sequences now begins with the player moving the ball with the inside instep to the right or left in the line of cones, this action supports the technical and physical foundation for the next working sequence. On reaching the end of the line of cones player A will apply 'The Forward Touch' (solid arrow) to move the ball forward (away from the line of cones) towards the shape in front of the line of cones. On the right side of the format player A can work on the simple option of moving the ball off the line against one defender (on the right) or the more complicated movement pattern against the two defenders (on the left).

From a development point of view the shape has to reflect on the players' needs. The main line of cones adheres to the development of the strength and technique of moving the ball with the inside instep to the left or right of the first or second challenger. The training function therefore takes care of both the physical and the technical side of the practice equation.

On the left - D1 and D2 represent the position of the first and second covering player (the possible covering positions). Player A practices moving the ball off the line against the first and second challenger for the ball.

On the right - The five-cone short line placement here represents the simple practice of moving the ball against a single opponent. The second part of the overall structure of the format, therefore, allows the player to practice moving the ball off the line against one or two defenders.

Any sequence of touches on the ball must include the 'head up' requirements and the ability to combine the use of a passing option to the service player. The objective of this format now includes interactive play with SP. This sequence will enable the player to combine and link up the relevant playing options which will enable him to deal with opponents effectively.
For example -

(a) Learning to link up different skills
(b) Learning to move correctly in relation to the opponent.
(c) Learning to keep square on to the action
(d) Learning to work the ball to the left and right of opponents
(e) Learning to keep the head up

Passing & Finishing - The above explanation of the foundational training format sets out the stall for understanding the training concept. Skills such as the drag back or sweep of the ball are different from the pass itself. The skill of passing the ball is a separate issue and therefore needs to be looked at in its own right. In terms of player development, the working formats as I have said before will look at a wide range of playing problems. One such problem will of course be the ability to pass the ball and to work with other players. The continuation of the practice sequence can end up with a pass to another player. The ability to pass the ball is also an essential part of playing soccer and it goes without saying that the art of passing the ball should also play an integral part in any training format. The good news here is that in many respects the art of passing the ball is simple to coach.

There are times in soccer where a particular skill can be used to create different playing effects. One such skill or set of skills is the pass. The pass can be made in numerous ways to create different playing effects. It's easy to understand the difference between the pass and the strike of the ball that scores a goal. The difference between passing the ball and finishing lies in the intent and not the technique. It can be said that the 'pass with an attitude' can become a finishing strike, it is that simple. The ability to pass the ball or to finish well is vital to the player. It should be noted that the successful development of the player is also measured by the quality of his passing and finishing ability. Here are examples of the working formats that concentrate on the development of these skills. Once again the development of the passing technique will come in handy when the work includes interactive movements with other players.

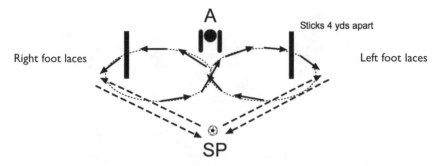

The Two - Stick Format - You won't believe how simple is it to teach the difference between striking the ball with the laces part of the boot and playing the ball with the inside instep. The actual technique of passing the ball is developed according to two basic body positions. The playing position requirements that are fundamental in the technique of passing and striking the ball are simple to define. The basic body position is as follows -

(a) Leaning away from the pass/strike - Use the laces
(b) Upright - Use the inside instep

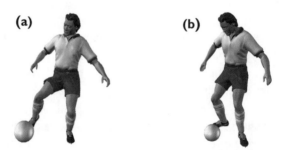

Points Of Reference - The instructions in the technique of passing the ball could not be made more easily than this; If the player is leaning his body away from the ball, he needs to apply the laces to the ball. If, on other hand, he has his body in an upright position (standing up straight) in relation to the ball, the ball should be played with the inside instep of the foot. The above format is designed to allow the player to begin to understand how to use his body in relation to the pass. The working pattern around the sticks in a figure eight run is designed to enable the player to play the ball as it comes from a leaning body position. The pass is made on the move, which teaches the pass and move habit. On the left side- Player A will round the stick on that side and play the ball diagonally to SP with the left boot (laces). If he rounds the stick on the right side, the return pass to SP will be made with the right boot (laces). The pass back to SP is made on the so-called first contact with the ball. The practice is continued on the move and player A works to a set repetition: 10 return passes - next player in.

Example explanation - The pass back is made on the move to as the player rounds the stick. The leaning body position takes place naturally here because the player has to round each stick from the back. The circles highlight the 'FIGURE EIGHT' movement. The figure eight run brings the player to the correct physical position for the return pass with the laces of the boot to SP. The length of the return pass is about ten yards. Tell the player to change his pace of work 'off the pass'. By this I mean sprint after the pass (move/sprint).

The Difference In Playing Techniques - It is important to enable the player to understand the difference between the pass made with the laces part of the boot and the inside instep. By the same token it is also important to teach the player the difference between an upright body position and the 'Leaning' body position in relation to the pass. The main reason for that has everything to do with the fact that it is the body position in relation to the ball and the foot to the ball position that makes all the difference to the outcome. The pass can be accurate or miss the intended target altogether if the player uses his body incorrectly in relation to the ball or if he fails to follow through on contact with the ball.

The Upright Body Position - In this next format the pass and move theme continues and the figure eight running pattern is same. However, in this next format the player will be encouraged to get into an upright body position when he comes into contact with the ball. To achieve that objective, instead of moving the body to the outside of the sticks, as shown above, the player will now move his body through the sticks that are placed to form a gate at either side of the format. When working to the figure eight run pattern the player simply moves his body through and between the 'two sticks'. As player A moves through the sticks, he will move naturally into an upright body position which will facilitate the application of the inside instep to the ball. He will move through the sticks and pass the ball to SP with the inside instep of the right foot or left foot (depending on which side of the format) -Player A passes and moves to the other side again as shown.

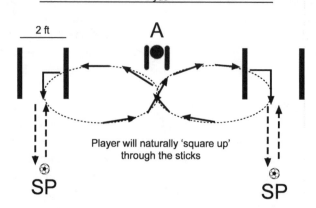

The reason for the sticks - The sticks create a natural movement structure that ensures the understanding of the function of the body in relation to the ball and therefore the pass. In moving through the sticks the player achieves an upright body position that enables him to play the ball with the inside instep from a square on body position. The starting position and the running pattern ensure the development of the correct attitude to the pass and therefore of the quality of the pass itself.

The Practice - In order to practice playing the ball back with the inside instep you need to position one service player with a ball on the left and right side of the format. On the left 'SP1' plays the ball to the player's right foot and on the right 'SP' plays to the left foot. It is important for the player to appreciate and understand the effects of the follow through (of the foot) on contact with the ball. This practice format includes the skill of looking up to see the target for the pass and the pass back to SP. Looking up takes place as the player moves through the gate. The player will, by virtue of working out in this way, quickly learn all about the effects of having to play the ball on the move and what it takes to hit the target if the technique of passing the ball is correct or incorrect. A good pass will be obvious.

Moving On - The working elements (skills) that I have explained thus far form the basis for the player's needs in terms of his basic develop-ment. Once the player is competent at passing the ball he will be ready to move on and try something a little more difficult. It is important to realize that the development of a good first touch and the pass and other skills are in fact worked on everyday. It is only when the player is competent at playing the ball with the inside instep or laces that he can tackle the higher standard formats. The development of the strength in the legs for passing the ball and for moving the ball to the lateral angle comes naturally from practicing, but there is a foot position that requires additional help.

The Inside Instep Foot Position - The inside instep to the ball position is unnatural and many players, especially the very young players, find it difficult to position the inside instep to the ball. One reason for that is a lack of inner groin strength. Taking the ball up on the inside instep from the air is a case in point. Here is a simple example of an exercise that enables the player to work on the inside instep outturned foot position. It is possible to use the following simple exercise in conjunction with the inside instep work done in the Straight line of cones. The additional help will keep the tendons supple and help the player achieve the inside instep foot position that is essential to the inside instep pass technique. This simple exercise is called the 'groin kick - backs'.

GROIN KICK BACKS

'SP' Throws the ball.

Player A kicks the ball back to the thrower with the inside instep part of the boot to the ball.

Instructions - SP throws the ball to the player and catches the return pass. The practicing player works on passing the ball back to SP by playing the ball back with the inside instep of the right and left foot respectively. SP throws the ball to the inside instep of the left and right foot alternately.

A POSITIVE APPROACH TO TRAINING

The scoring of goals requires the implementation of individual and team soccer skills, skills that must enable every player, no matter what their position, to move the ball in a creative way. I have always believed that the success of the team depends on the ability of the individual. In general terms - The more playing options a player has, the better the opportunity he has to create the right playing solutions. To win any game of soccer, you need every player to have the ability to take charge of his playing options. A winning team must be based on quality in every position on the pitch if they are to be successful. The following examples are working formats that cater to the development of the correct individual and therefore team attributes. The working formats show the way to a winning attitude that enables each player to -

(a) **Keep the ball** - don't give the ball away cheaply
(b) **Play effectively** - create playing options that have positive outcomes
(c) Never be afraid to **share possession** of the ball
(d) **Play unselfishly** - give the ball to a better positioned player
(e) Make **fewer mistakes** than anyone else.
(f) **Not give the ball away** through a lack of ability
(g) Play very well in the **'Attacking and Defensive'** phases

In simple terms - All of the above attributes come through as the player develops his physical and technical abilities. The stronger and more skilful the player, the better the player. It is that simple. It is a matter of getting the overall development of the player correct because this creates the type of player that has all the right attributes to be effective. It is not a question of strength without technique, or technique without strength, both must go hand in hand if you want to achieve higher standards of play. I am sure that in principle everyone agrees with that.

Playing The Game - What I would like to do now is to show and explain in a practical way the difference between a "drill" and any of my working formats. In this explanation of the training philosophy the drill part of the diagram is the run with the ball, the cross and the finish.

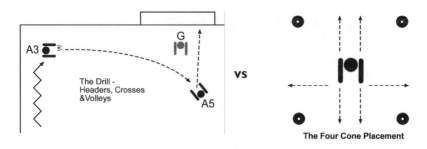

A3

G

The Drill -
Headers, Crosses
&Volleys

A5

vs

The Four Cone Placement

In simple terms the run and the cross represent a drill. The four-cone placement here represents the lateral concept. The difference lies in the need to define a working skill before you apply it to a playing solution. The four-cone placement and many lateral examples enable the player to define and develop the skills prior to their use in drills. The physical and technical ability to do the skills involved in the performance of even the most simple tasks must be taught prior to their use. The breakdown of the playing elements is based on what happens when the player takes up the ball in any playing scenario. In the above example, Player A3 runs and crosses the ball to player A5 who heads the ball home.

The difference - The drill represents the existing ability of the player to perform different skills, whereas working formats such as the four-cone placement represent the actual development of the skills in question that may be used in any drill scenario.

In other words, there is a need to look at the individual skills of soccer in their own right. It is not a question of lobbing everything into the pot and hoping things will turn out ok! They will not. In soccer development, nothing can be left to chance and you need to work on a wide variety of skills. Sometimes the actual training format can be very simple. Learning to run with the ball is one such example.

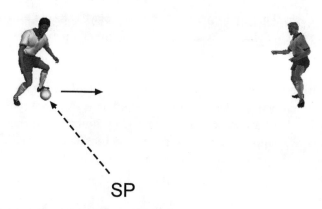

SP

Running off 'The Forward Touch'

In keeping with the explanation of the skills needed to organize a working format, running is an integral part of the training equation. There are of course different forms of running and the example shows one of the simplest of all. In the above example player A on the left receives the ball from SP - Player A receives the ball on the inside instep of the left foot and moves the ball forward and exchanges the ball with the next man in (next runner) in a special way. If the ball is kept on the right foot during the run, player A leaves the ball on the right foot of the next runner, and vice versa.

Alternatively - Return the pass to 'SP' - SP plays the ball back to the runner, thus completing what is known in the business as a 'one-two'. The player continues to run with the ball to the next man in and so on.

When Running - Some players are comfortable running with the ball by knocking the ball forward with the laces part of the boot, some are not. Running with the ball has always been a problem for some players because most players will always have to fight off the natural running foot position. The actual foot position on contact with the ball can be left up to the individual to choose his preference.

The Long Ball - Passing
Oddly enough, the long pass is something that players don't do naturally because most of the passes in the game are made short. However, the skill of playing the ball long is just as important as any other. I have often used long pass practice to break up the training session, especially when the training session was physically challenging. The long pass com-

pletes the basic skill requirements that every player should know. The practice format would not be complete without the players having the ability to play a thirty or more yard pass.

The Practice - Position the players fifty or so yards from each other. Begin with each player taking control of the ball from the air off the long pass. The ball can be controlled by taking the ball with the inside instep - see the simple groin exercise for the technique of taking the ball up on the inside instep. The long pass is played with the laces part of the boot.

Note - The goalkeeper comes in handy when you work on finishing and other movement concepts that end with a finish. I will not be able to explain this topic here but there are many books written on this subject by ex- goalkeepers who are well versed in the art of goalkeeping. I will, however, point any goalkeeper in the direction of my formats on feet coordination and the lateral movement formats. Some of the lateral formats are ideal for developing the goalkeeper's sideways stride movements and his kicking strength.

We talked about the need to understand the difference between the skills and their use. From a coaching point of view, this is a crucial issue. The interpretation of the first touch on the ball (first contact on the ball) can mean different things, mostly because there are different 'soccer' reasons for playing the ball. The meaningful first touch options that I have described have everything to do with the player using the space available around him in relation to his playing options. The proper first touch on the ball can make a huge difference in solving playing problems.

A SEPARATE ISSUE

Learning to take a meaningful touch to the ball does not at first glance appear to be the most complicated coaching issue, simply because the taking of a specific touch can be standardized. However, the simplicity of learning how to take the first touch to the ball does not in my opinion include the conditioned method of training. Please understand that even if a player knows only two of the first touch options covered in this book, he would be able to play soccer more effectively.

Question - What is the definition of a first touch option? It is certainly not just that the foot comes into contact with the ball. If a player takes a meaningless touch to the ball, one that does not take into account the play situation and subsequent playing options, then he has simply stopped the ball, nothing more.

The Two Touch Myth

This may come as a shock, but conditioning a game of soccer to two touches of the ball does more harm than good when working on developing the first touch if players are not trained specifically for the various first touch options beforehand. Without the skills and vision required to take a meaningful first touch (one that puts the ball into a playable position for the next touch), players will not develop and will continue to take "what for?" touches, simply stopping the ball.

A 'First' touch on the ball is but a single playing solution, one of many. Those coaches who believe in the battling attributes have failed to recognize some of the above points of reference and still promote the use of the conditioned game of soccer to develop the first touch. It is far better to approach the development of the player for the pass and move game by making sure that he is able to use the space around him more effectively. To do that, the coaching concept has to deliver more than the conditioned game of soccer.

There are good reasons why the conditioned game of soccer is a waste of time when it comes to developing a good first touch. If the player is off-balance his body position will not enable him to do much with his second touch, and even when he is balanced he is apt to take a bad touch because he has not been trained to make that second touch a meaningful one. Both problems occur often in conditioned games of soccer with players who have not had specific training for first touch options. There are also serious technical reasons in terms of developing the technique of playing the ball to a meaningful first touch (on the ball) that cannot possibly be achieved by the conditioned game of soccer. Basic first touch options need to be worked on separately and learned in a special way, a way that needs to consider the use of special working dimension/formats, formats that enable the player to develop his awareness of space and playing distance.

The following cone placement exercises are designed to develop the proper first touch options:

The Two and Three Cone Placements

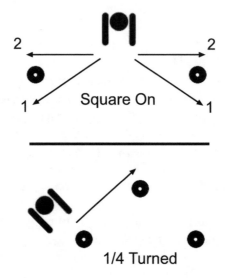

Simple but relevant - The simplicity of these formats on paper and on the practice ground may be misleading. They are, in fact, fundamental to the understanding of the first touch. The reason for the practice implications has everything to do with the relationship between the player and the position of the cones. When the player takes a touch on the ball to the angles shown in the above two and three cone placement formats he creates a soccer playing solution. The first touch options on view are called 'The Set Up Touch' (1) and the all - important skill of 'Moving The Ball Off The Line' (2). These touches on the ball enable the player to begin to use the playing space effectively. The accuracy of the touches is based on the fact that the safest touch on the ball in the game of soccer is made with the inside instep. The right foot inside instep moves the ball to the player's left and the left foot inside instep moves the ball to the player's right. The first touch is practiced to the angles shown by the format. The details on the technical aspects of play will be given later.

The Three Cone Placement - Knowing how to position physically to take a touch is part of the skill of playing and the ¼ turned body position as shown by the three cone placement is an example of that. The ¼ turned body position enables the player to work the ball to a '180 degree' angle, to both the left and the right. The playing of the ball to the angle shown is called playing the ball off the line with depth. In the above example, player A will move the ball off the line with the inside instep of the right foot. This skill is very effective when confronted by an on-coming challenger for the ball. To achieve the practice of the skills in question player A is positioned as you see him, first facing the ball in the two - cone placement and then ¼ turned in the three cone placement. The service comes from a position directly in front of the practicing player.

What Does All of This Imply? - In simple terms, all fundamental first touch options are defined by the playing direction, length of touch (distance the ball travels) and the angle of play. What makes these formats special is the way the player works with the ball. In all formats the player is taught to move on the touch but in a specific way. It is important to learn how to use the body in relation to the application of the consequential touch options. The most important of all the body shapes in terms of playing the skills in question is of course 'The 'Square On' body position. The 'Square On' body position (facing the pass) forms the technically correct playing platform for executing the first touch. The effective control of the ball comes from the ability to keep the upper body firm on the touch and square on to the action, while moving the foot to the direction of the touch.

The 'four cone' placement enables the player to work on playing the first touch options to a full 360 - degree angle. The complete set of first touch fundamental formats consists of -

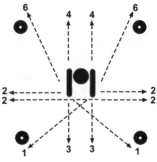

The Four Cone Placement

(a) The Two - Cone Placement
(b) The Three Cone Placement
(c) The Four - Cone Placement

These in turn enable the player to develop the first touch.

The resulting first touch options are played with the inside instep of the right or left foot respectively; The respective first touch options are:

1 - The Set Up Touch
2 - Moving the ball off the line
3 - The Forward Touch
4 - The Reverse Touch
5 - The Dink Touch (not shown)
6 - The Reverse Roll Touch
7 - Moving the ball off the line with depth (Three Cone Placement)

The above format shows the possible angles of escape on the first touch of the ball. In terms of the ability to play the first touch options the development of the physical strength on both sides of the body has never been more apparent than here. It is, therefore, once again worth pointing out the connection between the straight line of cones and other lateral training formats. Formats like the straight 'line of cones' are fundamental to the development of the first touch because the player learns to develop his lateral strength (the square on body position to the ball) and the feel/touch for the ball. The inside instep foot position/feel and strength of touch are attributes that are essential to a good first touch on the ball. Of course, there are numerous other reasons for developing a decent first touch on the ball.

Playing Off The First Touch - Every player should know how to play 'off the first touch' if he wants to keep possession of the ball. However, this can only be done effectively if the player possesses a meaningful first touch in the first place. Formats like the 'The four - Cone placement' are fundamental to such issues. In addition to the ability of how to play the first touch and play 'off' the first touch, there are also considerations of how to move with the ball against the first challenger or the covering player that need attention. It is of course a matter of knowing the movements and the skills in question.

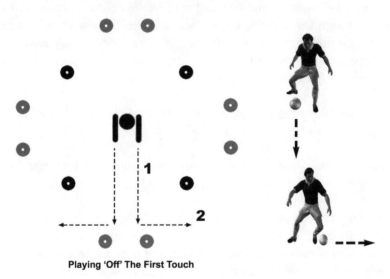

Playing 'Off' The First Touch

The four-cone placement forms the centerpiece of the above format. The cones to the outside represent the second touch phase of the practice. Hence the name 'The playing 'off the first touch' format.

Skill points of reference - In the above format, the practice endeavors are all about playing 'off' the first touch. The position of the cones to the outside of the main four - cone placement structure enable the practicing player to work on and develop the correct physical evasive movements with the ball that help the player keep the ball away from any challenging opponent.

The Working Principles - The way the above format works from a playing point of view and therefore in terms of soccer training can be explained in the following way. Imagine that you are about to take charge of the ball and the ball is coming to you from a pass made by one of your own team players. The ball arrives at your feet and you take up the ball on the first touch in a manner that sends the ball in front of you but suddenly you have an opponent trying to get in your way and take the ball. What do you do? The answer to that has to be that you go around the opponent and avoid him. The cones placed to the outside of the main four - cone placement structure are there to enable the player to practice avoiding the opponent just after taking the first touch. There are special one on one skills available to the player that he will need to know in order to be successful at going past the opponent with the ball. The cone placements to the outside of the format can be re-designed to enable the player to work on different playing problems. (See the first and second defenders cone placement position given earlier as an example)

Arrow 1 - Taking the first touch - The forward touch with the inside instep, practice with the right and left foot.

Arrow 2 - Taking the touch that moves the ball off the line laterally. Practice taking the touch with the right and left foot alternatively.

Changing The Shape Of The Format - When the format changes and the player is forced to deal with additional cone placements to the outside of the main structure, the touch and pass sequence can also change. In the above format the player learns to keep the ball to a minimum of three touches in any working sequence, with the exception of the reverse touch. The reverse touch poses the player different practice problems because in turning away with the ball from the service player, the pass back has to be made from an entirely different set of physical movements.

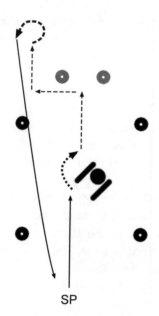

The Reverse Touch - The foot in contact with the ball cushions the pass as the player turns to follow the ball.

SP

For Example - When the player works on the 'Reverse Touch', the sequence could be as follows; 1 - Player A takes a reverse touch and turns with the ball away from the service player - 2 - Player A moves the ball off the line against the back set of cones - 3 - Player A plays the forward touch to move the ball beyond the set of cones (opponent) - 4 - Player A makes a 180 degree turn to face the service player - 5 - Player A takes a touch that sets the ball up for a pass back to the service player - 6 - Player A makes the pass back to the service player - 7 - Player A takes up his position again to receive the next pass from SP.

The body position - Once a first touch is taken to the ball to any direction shown it is vital that player A develops his ability to keep the body position upright and 'Square on' off the touch as soon as possible. The cones placed outside of the main structure (the four cone placement) to the four working directions are there to enable the player to practice getting the body shape upright 'Off' any selected first touch option. In terms of the actual body language, the 'Square on' and upright body position allows the player to move to any direction and the outside cones are there to help the player develop his upper body movements in relation to the touch. In the above format example, the attacking player (the player on the ball) can also practice the body movements that help him to send the opponent in the wrong direction. For example - Dropping the shoulder to the left and moving off with the ball to the right and vice versa.

Note - The challenge for the ball can come from any direction, so being able to find escape routes and move the ball to any direction is vital to maintaining possession. The above format takes into account the probable position of the challenger in the opponent's team structure (the playing system).

Compelling Reasons - Take into account that it is not possible for any player to run for an entire training session because you will not be able to sustain the concentration or the will to work. The working formats, on other hand, enable the player to spend a greater amount of time on the ball, working out on the skills in question because these are condensed playing formats. In other words, these simulate game conditions but without the rigors of the game. The players can work on different playing movements without getting tired and bored with practice. This is a serious issue because improvements to the player's overall playing abilities depend on practice. Of course, it is not just a question of how many touches a player can take during a practice session, but how many of those touches constitute 'Quality Time' on the ball. The coaching objectives of the above format enable the coach to control what takes place more effectively. For example, the coach can -

(a) Keep an eye on how the player moves with the ball.
(b) Concentrate and target the development of specific skills.
(c) Ensure that the players practice correctly.
(d) Ensure that the players keep their concentration.
(e) Keep the training interesting.
(f) Keep the player from overworking.
(g) Ensure variety of work more easily.

In keeping with the reality that there are playing scenarios during free play that dictate how many touches the player takes to the ball, my formats make it possible for the player to experience the movements in a practical manner. The resulting effect of the above practice format enables the player to:

1 - Recognize standard playing moments.
2 - Apply standard playing solutions.
3 - Develop alternative playing solutions

The choreography formats recognize the need to keep things realistic and the cone placements are reflective of the angles related to keeping possession of the ball and the technical requirements for dealing with many playing problems. Yes, there are playing scenarios that are solved by the application of two touches, but what touches and how they are played is an important issue.

What Is A Standard Playing Solution?

**The Pass on
First Contact**

Standard Playing Options - There should be absolutely no doubt that in certain play situations, a player receiving the ball will have no choice but to pass the ball quickly on first contact. The point is that there are indeed standard playing solutions to standard playing problems. The above example demonstrates that simply and clearly. It is also right to assume that the above example represents nothing more than a single playing problem with one playing solution.

**The Three-Touch
Playing Scenario**

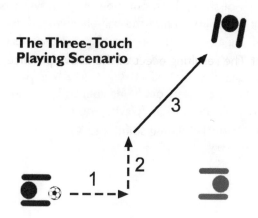

The Standard Playing Moment -

A standard playing moment can take one, two, or three touches to the ball. In the above example, the player changes his mind and veers away from the option of taking on the defender, deciding instead to implement another playing solution rather than risk losing possession of the ball. The player on the ball takes the touch that moves the ball off the line - See touch (2) This touch is made with the inside instep of the right foot - The left foot plays the ball to the direction shown by arrow 3. Technically speaking, arrow 3 could also show the pass that can be played with the outside of the right boot. These are simple playing situations that prove the existence of a standard playing option. The standard playing options in the above examples utilize the following skills-

    1 - Taking a forward touch
    2 - Moving the ball off the line
    3 - Playing the pass with the laces or outside of the foot

Standard options do exist and thus so does the need for the choreography of 'Soccer' for practical reasons. The skills we have discussed have been effectively translated into the above cone placement formats. The above numbers 1 and 2 represent the forward touch and the off the line touch. These skills are worked on in the two and four - cone placement formats. The pass shown by arrow 3 in the above diagram is a separate coaching issue that I will cover in a later chapter on passing. The skills in question and the pass are combined to create the above playing solution.

Understanding The Make Up Of The Skill - It is vital to understand that the lack of strength on one side of the player's body is a disaster in terms of his ability to play the ball effectively. If the body is weak on one side as a result of poor training, the player's chances of holding the 'square on' body position and therefore playing the first touch options to any direction effectively is greatly impaired. A quality standard performance comes from being able to keep the body 'Square On' to the ball when receiving and playing the ball. It is essential to have a balanced lateral strength in order to play to any direction and use both feet effectively.

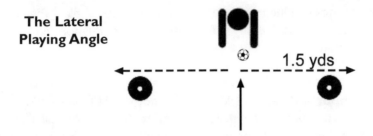

The Lateral Playing Angle

1.5 yds

In Technical Terms - The lateral angle in the above two - cone placement (and in the four - cone placement shown earlier) establishes certain skill factors and movement factors that cannot be ignored. The development of the lateral playing ability (playing the ball to the lateral angle) ensures the correct physical development of the player. 'First and foremost' it is the definition of the skills that makes all the difference to their acquisition and to the quality of their performance. Player A is positioned behind two cones placed 2 yds apart. His central position allows him to take a touch of about 1.5 yds in length past the cone to either side of his position. Facing the pass from SP, Player A practices taking the ball with the inside instep of the boot. The right foot moves the ball to the left and the left foot moves the ball right. Move the ball to the 'Square on' angle shown but do it in a way that moves the foot in contact with the ball to the direction of the touch and keep facing the service player. This touch is simply called 'Moving the ball off the line', a defined touch that is essential to the game of soccer.

It is one thing to demonstrate a particular skill and another thing entirely to expect any player to perform what he has been shown. There are so few skills in use today because it is virtually impossible for any player to learn a skill by simply watching someone else perform it and also many of the skills taught are not part of the standard playing repertoire. Most players who have no idea what skills form the standard skills of soccer end up playing their own favorite skill and nothing more. The 'lack of time' on the ball often results in players keeping to a simple pass and move way of playing.

Keeping The Game Simple

The worst possible reason for a lack of skills is a belief in a certain way of playing that reduces the need for a wide variety of playing solutions. Players who practice indoors during the winter months are also less likely to apply defined skills due to the tight areas of play, where the time on the ball is fleeting. Young players in that situation tend to use skills that are familiar and easy to use, shying away from the risk involved in trying anything new.

The Important Issues - If a player is not taught how to take a decent first touch, he will never develop to his full potential. The acquisition of skills through the use of practice formats does not produce a style of play but an ability to play soccer. The purpose of the practice formats is simply to enable the player to produce the skills that will solve any playing problem. How the player plays and to what style depends on the problems that come up during play. The playing standards are raised effectively by the fact that the player possesses the ability to move the ball on the first touch in a meaningful way. That means that the player can and does play the appropriate touch option for a given play scenario without restrictions or inhibitions and applies his body precisely to what is required in order to solve any playing problem.

It is my contention that a practical working format helps the player to acquire the skills in question in less time than any other way of working. The defined method of training targets correctly the development of the skills and the physical side of the player to play the skills to any direction, with either the left or the right foot. The position of the player in any practice format is consistent with the practical reality of the game of soccer. It is simply not good enough to develop a player to only possess the ability to play the ball with his so-called good foot. It is vital to develop the player in a way that enables him to feel comfortable on the ball when using both the right and left foot because there are indeed playing events that require the use of one or the other foot. The linking up of different soccer playing elements in practice is essential to the development of a player's playing repertoire. The practical objectives of the formats, therefore, include endeavors in areas of play such as -

(a) The player's ability to combine the utilization of different movements - skills
(b) The player's ability to apply the skills in question to form a winning attribute.

The overall training development program, therefore, is obviously designed to target a wide range of player attributes.

Obviously, you may have already guessed that there are different forms of soccer fitness training which require the application of appropriate forms of training. The skill formats and the first touch exercises will obviously cater to the type of fitness required for moving the ball in a skilful way. However, in terms of other physical endeavors such as running and sprinting without the ball or reaction training you will need to work on those issues in exercises that target them specifically.

Physical Fitness

The ability to play soccer is based on fitness training and technical training. Since the physical development and the technique development goes hand in hand it is only correct to begin the explanation of the soccer skills involved by first looking at the fitness side of the training equation. The word 'Fitness' may be used to describe the physical requirements for playing soccer, but there are in fact many different forms of fitness. For example, consider the body as a system of muscle forms, in that case player (A) needs to work on and possess fitness for:

- **Moving with and without the ball** - Leg to ball coordination
- **Agility** -The ability to jump, turn and twist - with and without the ball.
- **'Man on' Battling attributes** for competition.
- The **'Quality'** of performances
- The ability to **keep possession** of the ball in tight areas of play.
- **Stamina** - Staying power - Running forms and Special Circuit Workouts.

Weight Training or Lateral Formats?

The Secret - The ability to play soccer effectively does not come from working out with weights without specialized attention. I acknowledge the fact that the weight training room has its use but only for developing the upper part of the body and only with specialized forms of training. The legs do not need the weight training room for several reasons. Weight training has the effect of compromising a player's agility and suppleness, qualities that are essential in moving correctly or effectively with or without the ball. The difference between my routines and the weight training workout lies in the fact that my formats create what can be described as kinetic tension. Kinetic tension is a natural source of energy and, therefore the generated strength that results from the formats helps the player to develop the ability to move the ball far more effectively than by pumping iron. Understand this - lateral formats develop the correct muscle and body strength composition to play soccer effectively. It is not a question of having a big body and the strength of a lion but little or no stamina or playing skills on the ball.

Soccer fitness training formats have a job to do and that function is to develop the physical movements that are found in the game:

(a) **Walking** - There is a certain amount of walking during the game and this is catered to within the working formats.
(b) **Jogging** - Once again, there is a certain amount of jogging taking place and this has to be a part of any training session.
(c) There are different forms of **running** that need to be considered: Half pace, 3/4 pace, Sprints, Shuttle,
(d) **Reaction** forms of training: Check outs, changes in running direction etc -
(e) Mental fitness - Concentration forms of training.

Most training sessions will have to acknowledge the fact that during play the player will most certainly implement a lot of changes to the pace of his/her running and to the length of run
and, to the direction of the players run and, to the length of stride taken. For those reasons there has to be different ways of achieving soccer fitness. Here is a very simple example that we all know about where the working criteria of (a to c) can be used to form a working fitness training sequence, for example -

The amount of running in each section can be determined to reflect the effort required, for example: Sprints - 50 yds , 3/4pace - 100 yds, jog - 150 yds, walk - 200 yds. All such considerations depend of course on other factors such the age of the player. It is obvious that young children cannot be expected to perform to the same working criteria as older players. As far as the younger players are concerned you will obviously need to reduce the amount of effort in terms of reps or distance shown. As is always the case it is quite possible to work on each section separately. In addition, it is possible to combine some of the above fitness solutions with other working formats.
On the other hand - Here is a new but simple idea for an exercise to change the length of the player's stride.

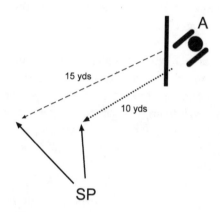

15 yds

10 yds

A

SP

The Format - Position player A as shown behind the stick and a service player (SP) to one side of the stick to pass the ball to him. On each service of the ball the player jogs back to the starting position. In practice you will find that when player A rounds the stick to come to the short pass from SP, he will use a short stride. On the other hand, if the ball is played long by SP, player A will naturally take a longer stride to make that longer run. The job of player A is to respond to the service of the ball by moving out quickly to the ball wherever it is played. In that case player A will either run with a short stride or a longer stride depending on the length of the pass. Simple! Since the principles of the work here are similar to the shuttle run, there will be a fatigue factor and the duration of the practice should be considered carefully.

Understanding the running stride

Running in a straight line is easy, or so you would think. But in the reality of the game this is not the case. Most players can't run properly because they spend a lot of time using the shorter stride due to the fact that quite a lot of soccer movements are short in length. The biggest mistake anyone can make in developing a player's running stride for pace is to only work the player down a straight line of cones. The development of pace comes from working in a variety of exercises. The shuttle run is part of the working equation but not the only exercise involved.

By getting the player to run down the line of cones you can work on improving his stride alignment, but there is, as always, more to stride and pace development than that. You need to know the whole picture if you are to develop "soccer" pace.

In the single line of cones format the player will indeed learn to place one foot in front of the other in a better stride pattern, but there is a downside to working exclusively with that format. When the player moves his feet in this way from one gap to the next down the line of cones, he is essentially developing his short stride pattern because the feet are moving relatively close to the ground and the stride is short in length. This type of training, if not supplemented with other types of run technique training, will have the effect of shortening the running stride. The correct way of working on developing the different running abilities is to make sure that the physical and technical balance is always looked at from every angle. In other words, it is vital to know the effects of each exercise from a positive and not so positive (the negative) perspective in order to counter the down side of any exercise. What needs to be done is to counter the above short length of stride exercise by employing another working format that will balance the training by developing the ability to lengthen the stride when necessary. I gave a simple example of how to work on the change of stride pattern previously. The following exercise is specifically designed to counter the effects of the low foot lifts.

'The Circle Format'
The following circle format is designed to enable the player to develop a high knee lift. The high knee lift practice format does two important things for the player: 1 - The high knee lifts develop strength in the thigh and calf. 2 - The high knee lifts result in a longer length of stride capability. The strength for running comes from the kinetic intensity of the work generated from moving the body around the inner circle. The foot lifts result in a stronger push-off capability for sprinting action.

The High Knee Lift Format

The Circle Format - To develop the stride -

In the above format the player skip/jump/strides over the tape, one foot leading all of the time to either a counter-clockwise or clockwise direction. When working around the circle the player needs to make sure that the movements of the stride/jumps around the circle are performed on the toes and not on heels. The movements within the format should be performed to a good rhythm without a pause. The practice effort should not last for more than about 30 to 60 seconds or be set to more than 3 to 5 complete circles for best effect. If you are working on strength and stamina use the circle as part of the 'Match Play' fitness circuit and do 2 reps per leading leg before moving to the next exercise (see circuit training examples).

Turning & Sprinting Short Distances

First To The Ball - Clearly there is a need to work on and develop different forms of movements related to running considerations because there are different reasons for running during a match. It is not just about being quick physically over short distances (anything from 2 to 7 yds or so) or longer distances. We must also work on being quick mentally, improving our ability to make decisions in seconds or even fractions of seconds. In other words, being first to the ball depends not only on physical speed but on quick decision making. Obviously, the faster the player thinks, the quicker he will react and the better the effect on the game.

The Shuttle Run

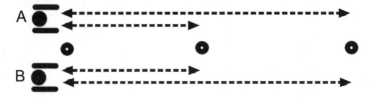

The shuttle run - Physically Quick - This is the simplest of all the working exercises on sprinting and turning technique. You can make the shuttle runs into a competitive format. Players A and B compete - run to each cone and back - The first man to go back and forwards to all the cones from the starting position to the finish line (starting position) wins, it is that simple.

Physical Considerations - Turning - on the (back foot) - It is worth pointing out that some players may prefer to turn back on the right foot (left shoulder) and others on the left foot (right shoulder) when reaching the cones to change the direction of the run. Work on both the left and right shoulder turn.

Turning

Defensively - It is worth practicing turning back on both the left and right shoulder. This is because there are times when the defender is already in a jockeying position and the decision on which way to turn will have been made for him by the attacking player's actions. Consider - If the attacking player goes past the defender on his open shoulder it easy for the defender to turn and move to the ball. On other hand - When the attacking player makes his attacking moves towards the leading shoulder of the defender it is harder for the defender to control the opponent's run with the ball. The main reason for that comes from the physical reality of having to turn around 'off' that shoulder position. Once the opponent goes past the defender's leading shoulder (the shoulder nearest to the attacking player) the defender will not be able to keep up with the attacking player. In a physically balanced (physically strong on both the left and right side) player, turning back to the right or left would not be a problem. The problems arise when the defender has been developed incorrectly and is physically weak on one side of his body. The player's weaker side will slow him down and make it difficult for him to turn effectively.

The Plant and Sprint Out Format - It is not that difficult to construct formats that develop the ability to turn the body quickly to the left or right.

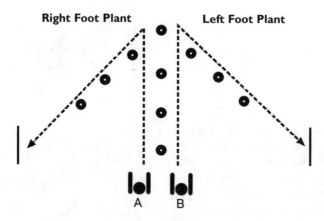

In this example player A and B compete to be the first man to get to and touch the stick. The skills of turning are -

(a) Turning 'off' the right foot (A). The left shoulder turns in the sprint-out direction.
(b) Turning 'off' the left foot (B). The right shoulder turns in the sprint-out direction.

Note - The best way to turn involves getting your feet to move to a shorter stride just before the turn. The sprint up to the turning point is made with a long stride, but as you approach the turning point the length of stride is greatly reduced to accommodate the turn. Players must not pause at the sharp end of the turning point. The turn is made with the 'The bracing leg'. The bracing leg is the leg nearest to the center run up line. Different turning possibilities come from working out in different formats - The shuttle sprint run has a full 180 degree turn whereas the turn above is made to the diagonal angle. The diagonal working angle here strengthens the player's ability to change the direction of his defensive run.

Attacking option 1 - Taking on the defender - Without cover - The defender (D) shows the blue attacking player to the left (down the touchline).

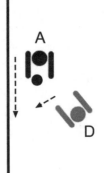

Attacking option 2 - Dribbling run against defenders - Covers on - The defender is showing player A to his right. If the defender has a defending partner he may be happy to show/jockey the attacking player onto the path of the second defender.

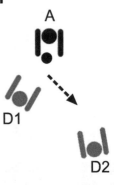

Good defenders don't just jump in like a bull in a china shop, they wait and try to win the ball when the time is right. The best way to defend is to jockey the attacking player into a bad attacking position. Getting the attacking player's head down so that he cannot see different playing options is always a priority. Once the attacking player's head is down and he is looking at the ball, his playing options are effectively reduced. It is at this point that the defender can force the attacking player into a playing situation where the ball can be won. The covering player's tactic can help the defending players with such objectives. It is a different matter when the attacking player is in control of the ball and the defender has little or no influence. In such situations the best thing to do is to be patient and wait for a bad touch. Keep in mind that good defensive tactics are based on things like jockeying and stealth and not on bone crunching tackles and challenges that some call defensive tactics. If you intend to kick someone in the name of defending you are merely cheating. There is nothing wrong with honest tackling, but there are honest endeavors to win the ball and there is dirty play. The game of soccer is not about kicking your way through to a winning position. This is something that, unfortunately for all of us who love the game, is a common practice.

Sometimes, the best defensive option is to give way. Giving way to the attacking player and still keeping the attacking player in check is very difficult. The following (jockeying) practice format enables the player to practice giving way by jockeying sideways and backwards. At some point in such a playing scenario the defensive movements may require the ability to change directions or body shape in response to the attacking player's change of direction. The following format works on fast defensive turns and changes in direction. Take a look at the way the player needs to practice the jockey defensive turns (moving through the line) and the lateral straddle movements against a fast moving attacker. Keep in mind that the jockeying skill has its limitations. The safest place/time to use this skill is when the first challenger for the ball has cover.

The Defensive Jockeying Format

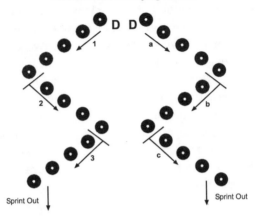

Describing the action:

1 = left shoulder down	a = right shoulder down
2 = right shoulder down	b = left shoulder down
3 = left shoulder turn and out	c = right shoulder turn and out.

In the above example the dotted lines between the cones represent the lateral jockeying movements. In the interest of the development of the technical side of the movements, the player should not touch the cones. The cones are only there to mark out the angles for practicing the lateral movements and body shape changes necessary to keep up with a new attacking direction. The cones are set up to mimic that game situation. Also, they are placed to reflect the size of the defender's shoulders, and for a very good reason. Moving the feet to the player's shoulder width promotes inner groin strength and therefore his overall lateral body strength. The movements and angles worked in this format will help prevent the player from getting caught flat footed and sent in the wrong direction when controlling the attacking run. Every player should learn to move the body both defensively and offensively and learn to work with the ball in an economical way. By economical I mean in a way that takes less touches on the ball and the right amount of physical movements to perform a given playing solution. Paying attention to details of this nature is vital for saving energy.

Learning To Appreciate Attacking & Defensive Angles - We all know that the direct route to goal affords the best chance of scoring a goal because it opens up more of the target (goal). However, running with the ball in a straight line has its implications. For one thing, when the ball is in front of the runner, it is in the wrong place for the player to get a decent strike or to avoid the oncoming defender. There are several things that can affect the attacking run. The first thing is obviously the influence of the defending player, the second is the angle of the run. Less obvious is the number of touches taken to the ball. Too many touches allows the defender more time to recover. The same is true if the attacking player takes too many wrong touches to the ball. We can assume that the same principles apply to the defender. If the defender, for example, takes the wrong approach to the attacking player he will not stop the attacking run. The defender has to counter what the attacking player does, but the clever attacking player can use the defensive counter tactics to his advantage.

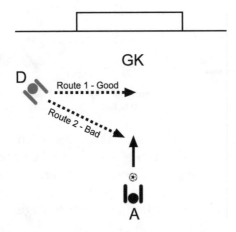

The simple answer as to why anyone should pay attention to such details should come from the realization that there is a right and a wrong way of doing things that can affect the outcome of any playing scenario. From a defensive point of view the defensive run 1 shows the proper approach line by the defender to this attacking line of player A. Route 2, on the other hand, shows the incorrect approach to the attacking run.

Once the defender moves into line with the attacking run he needs to take charge of the playing situation. The choreography practice solution, therefore, helps the defender to achieve that objective by making sure that the defensive movements are correct in relation to the attacking player's ability to perform his attacking objectives.

FIRST & FOREMOST

From a defensive point of view - The first job of the defender is to learn to move across the attacking player's path (Route 1 above). Getting between the goal and the ball (the attacking player) is a defensive priority. The defender should always face the action, so when making this movement to get into good defensive position, sideways straddle movements are the best option. This will keep the defender square on to the action and better able to limit the options of the attacking player.

Side Straddles - The Straddle Defensive Movements

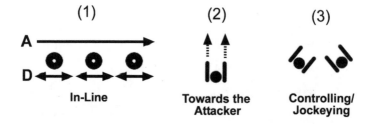

(1) **(2)** **(3)**

A

D

In-Line | Towards the Attacker | Controlling/ Jockeying

Moving Into A Defensive Posture - The above defensive options 1 to 3 will position the defending player in line with the opponent to hopefully block the attacking run. Once this sequence of movements is achieved the player shapes up to the angle that will either send the attacking player to the right or left of his intended target.

Note - The above diagrams show the movement sequence of a defensive player when lining up to address the attacking run. - 1 D - The defender moving to the lateral angle (in the following example checking out at times to re-assess the attacking run angle) 2 D - The defender moving forward, closing down the attacking players run and 3 D - Getting the body shape in place to win the ball.

Practice Counter Movements - As for the attacker, his run with the ball can be performed to any angle. From that point of view the jockeying format can also be used to have the attacking player practice his touch on the ball against a defender that gives way. When working in the next format the attacking player will be positioned to the other side of the (defender) jockeying player. The zig zag cone placement enables both the attacking player and the defensive player to practice moving the ball/body to the right and left of the attacking and defensive run. Once again, in the interest of physical balance, every player (both the attacking and the defending player) should get the opportunity to defend or to work the ball to the angles shown on both the right and left side.

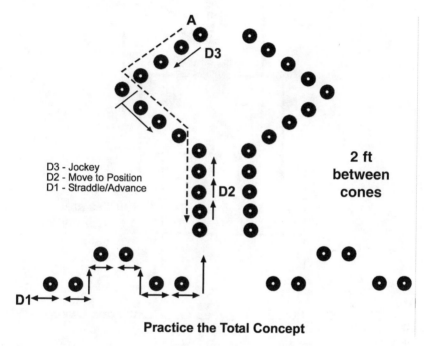

Practice the Total Concept

Working in pairs - It should be obvious that in this format the players can work in twos to practice the attacking and defensive duties on either side of the working format. When working in twos it is possible to have 'four players' working through the defensive and attacking theme at any one time. This is because it is possible for each player to begin the work on both the right and left side of the format. Players can swap roles after each working sequence has been completed.

The Agility Performance Back Up

There is a need to back up the technique development program by working on the development of the physical movements without the ball that are designed to help the player develop the strength to play the actual skills of soccer. The following example shows how to work on the lateral physical preparatory movements without the ball. The movements in the next format example are directly related to the skill of sweeping the underside of the boot across the ball.

The Physical Support - High Knee Lifts

Hurdles are 1 soccer ball high

The Skills - Left Foot Sweep and Right Foot Sweep

Physical strength - The sideways 'Lateral' jumps are designed to help the player develop his lateral physical strength and the body movements involved in the skill of moving the foot over the ball.

A POINT OF ORDER - Every working format is designed to develop the ability to play different soccer skills. Some formats are designed to target the development of a specific skill by working directly on the movements involved with the ball, while others target the development of the physical movements indirectly without the ball. The resulting strength on both the right and left side of the body that comes from working in the lateral forms of training is without doubt very useful to the player in all technical and physical endeavors. The most important of all training effects enables the player to keep the ball in a good playable position and under control at all times. This in turn gives the player better vision and better eye to ball coordination, which enables him to implement a wider range of playing options. That is the true legacy of the lateral formats.

What Is A 'Square On' Body Position?

The strong and physically balanced player can move the ball more effectively than a player who is weak on one side of the body because he can keep his body upright more readily and the ball in a playable position. The need for a balanced player is never more clear than when the player can't play the ball to any direction. In the lateral movement exercises it is the effort put into keeping the body 'Square on' to the action that is the key to improving the physical and technical skills of the player. Keeping the body square on to the action ensures the development of a better physical posture and that in turn enables the player to take a better touch to the ball.

When Strong Physically - The physically balanced player on the right in the above diagram can go to any direction of his choice. The physically weak player on the left can't do that and will always have problems when handling the ball on his first touch. The importance of keeping the ball in the right - place for playing different skills (not too close to the body and not too far away) is crucial in many technical respects - if the ball is in the right place, the player can:

(a) Play the ball to any direction
(b) Play the ball with both the right and left foot
(c) Play a wider range of skills
(d) Take on any defender more effectively
(e) Change directions more easily
(f) Play the ball as it comes, therefore play the ball quicker
(g) Change the playing options more easily

THE SKILLS FORMATS

The Change of Direction Format

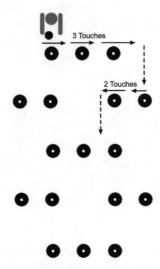

A BALANCE TEST FORMAT

The above format will expose the lack of balance in a player. One foot-ed players will find it hard to move the ball with the inside instep through this format and keep the body 'square on' to the action. If this is the case they cannot move the ball effectively with the left foot if they are right footed or the right if they are left footed, especially when a defender tries to take possession of the ball. This can easily be veri-fied by the above cone placement.

1 - Keep the 'LEFT SHOULDER' out of true and in position A2
2 - Keep The 'RIGHT SHOULDER' out of true and in position A1

TRUE   **A1**   **A2**

Physical Problems - If one side of the body is weaker than the other, that side of the body will always give way. That cannot be good from a playing point of view. The player will not be able to stay square on to the action, which will make it difficult for him to move in one or more of the playing directions we have already looked at.

The two-cone placement shows the angle that adheres to the principles of touch development and in fact represents the foundational steps in first touch development and the 'Square on' ability from a coaching point of view. All square on formats enable the player to work on and develop his ability to maintain a square on position on the first touch without collapsing the shoulder to the right or left of the action. The position of the cones and the working angle they represent is of great value to the technical development of the player. See the first touch options for more details.

Note - 'It is impossible to develop the lateral skills of soccer without the application of the lateral angle in different forms of training'

The work to this angle is the solution to -

1 - *The Lateral Physical Capability* - The development of the strength to play effective 'soccer'

2 - *The Technical Capability* - The development of the correct foot positions to the ball that bring about the ability to utilize the correct options.

3 - *The Development of a Playing Repertoire* - The variety of the work creates a source of skills that solves different playing problems.

Playing Options (Examples)

Option A - The Dink Touch
Can be used when the defender
lunges for the ball

Option B - Moving the Ball Off the Line
Creates playing space

The skill of moving the ball off the line is a simple example and yet from it is of great importance in keeping possession of the ball - In option A - The defender lunges in to win the ball. The solution is to 'Dink Touch' the ball over the opponent's foot. In option B, even though the defender is too far away to cause any immediate problems, the white player utilizes the skill of moving the ball off the line to open up his playing options.

The progressive nature of the working formats
In essence the work on the first touch options begins by first of all developing the short touch lateral ability in the straight line of cones. The development of the player is then improved by working in formats that allow him to develop the feel of playing the ball to the different lateral lengths of touch. There are two options that lay down the foundation for the development of touch.

Option 1 -   The short inside instep (straight line of cones)
Option 2 -   The long length of touch ('two-cone' placement)

In learning to distinguish between the two lengths of touch the player establishes the fundamental movements in playing the different skills of soccer. The development of the ability to play the ball to the different lengths of touch and directions of touch is a matter of working with the ball in the appropriate formats.

Skills Touch

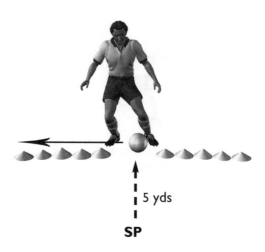

1 - Hold the body posture 'square on' and upright.

2 - Keep the shoulders square and parallel to the lateral angle

3 - Get into the habit of moving the foot on the touch before the upper body.

SP - Pass the ball between the right and left leg.

5 yds

SP

The above cone placement is representative of the position of the first challenger. Compare the open two - cone placement to the above format. The above example does not allow the player to work on the skill of setting the ball up for a pass. See first touch options for reference on 'The Set Up Touch'. In this format the angle to the set up touch is closed off. The main reason for this is based on the chronology of the formats. The shapes are important to the memory part of the training process and therefore each shape represents a different practice problem and subsequent playing solution. The above format shows the practical interpretation of play option 2 above as an example of how to utilize the skill of moving the ball off the line in order to open up the area of play. The overall working principles of the two - cone placement format enables the player to work on and develop his playing abilities in ways that are useful to his playing options.

1 - The player learns to play the correct length of touch
2 - The player learns to play the ball to a specific direction.
3 - The player learns to stay 'square on' on the touch
4 - The player develops the ability to look up off the first touch and set up the next touch.

The working formats, therefore, are not just about the development of the strength side of the player. These are also utilized for the purpose of teaching the player how to work the ball in difficult playing situations. In technical terms, keeping possession of the ball depends on a number of skills. Moving on the touch, for example, is an essential skill because the ability to do so creates technical results. For example -

1 - The first stride off for greater ball control
2 - A better range of playing options.
3 - Saves the player time and therefore energy.

Practical Experience

The practice environment - The above example shows a 1.5 yd cone placement (five cone width) to the right and left of the player. When the player is positioned behind the cones as shown he is able to 'move the ball off the line' with the inside instep of either foot to the angle and distance of the working guideline set by the cone placements. The ball is moved across the body of the player with the appropriate foot (inside instep) or by extending the foot to the ball and therefore playing the ball with the inside instep to the lateral direction of the touch. The ball is moved parallel along either the left or right side of the cone placements (the working format) - In this example the player moves the ball with the inside instep of his left foot to his right. As always: lots of follow through, moving the foot on the touch, keeping square on to the touch and moving the body to the direction of the touch. The five cone placements to the right and left side of the player represent a specific playing function. The cones to the right of the player denote the taking on of the defender on the defender's left shoulder, while the cone placements to the left of the player denote the practice of taking on the defender on his right shoulder.

Being a perfectionist - 'Being a perfectionist' should be thought of as 'Improving playing standards'. In reality, it is not possible to ignore the fact that most skills require a specific working sequence. Even in the so-called simple format of moving the ball off the line, the definition of the working sequence is there for no other reason than to help the player develop certain habits and attributes. For example -

The correct playing & Working habit sequence - When performing the first touch options, the player needs to keep to a specific working sequence if he wishes to improve his technical abilities.
For example -

The Playing Sequence

1 - look up
2 - Take charge of the ball (look down) and take a touch
3 - look up off the touch
4 - look back down and pass the ball.

The work on any single skill option takes place to the above practical playing working sequence. The working sequence therefore includes 'The pass' to the player from the service player. In addition to the above reference points the working sequence is made up of -

1 - The application of different first touch options
2 - The pass - Of varying length and height

From a technical point of view

The above single skill practice format concentrates on the practice of 1 - the first touch and 2 - the pass made with the inside instep. The sequence of movements in every sense is different to that of any simple conditioned 'two touch' game of soccer. This is because the above examples deliver a standard playing option that is defined by the **PHYSICAL MOVEMENTS**. The difference between conditioning the game of soccer to two touches of the ball and the above format lies in the definition of the make up of the skills involved. What interests me is not the philosophy behind the conditioned games of soccer but the make up of the skills. I personally worry about the players who practice soccer without understanding the nature of the skills involved. I know as a coach that any lack of skill definition is wrong and that the conditioned practice game to two unspecified touches actually obscures the difference between the different first touch options (see first touch options) available to the player. I also know that the lack of skill definition leads to a lack of attention in terms of understanding and developing the proper first touch options which are fundamental to the game of soccer.

The Ability To Combine Skill Options

The lack of definition - I would have to say that if a player does not understand the skills of soccer he will not be able to develop the ability to create a quality playing solution. Taking on more than one opponent, for example, requires the use of a number of skills. These have to be taught in a defined way if the player is to acquire the ability to play any of them effectively. Every player needs to be able to take up the ball (use the body) from any playing direction or problem, whether the ball comes on the ground or in the air. In terms of ball control, it is just as difficult to play the ball on the move as it is from a static position. The ability to play the ball effectively whatever the playing situation is the name of the game.

Reading The Game - The secret to success lies in the player having the ability to see what is happening in front of him 'first and foremost' and to then move the ball effectively in response to any decision he has made. The skill of reading the game and looking up and playing the ball to the correct working sequence is easier said than done. The two - cone placement is there to deal with such problems. One of the most un-natural things you can ask any player to do is to look up and assess things around him before he receives the ball. Most players don't assess their playing options until after they receive the ball. The correct way of working the ball in relation to playing options is to look up and see the playing options beforehand and then look down and take a touch to the ball. By assessing things, I mean assessing the whereabouts of both the opposition and teammates.

Looking up - The ability to assess the playing area beforehand is crucial to the selection of the correct action. When the player can note the position of his opponents before receiving the ball, he can take a touch that will send the ball to the direction that is free of any opponent, hence the need to develop the choice of specific first touch options.

Part 1- Reading The Game - Decisions - Which Touch?

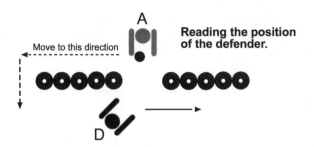

In practical playing terms - When taking on the first challenger for the ball, reading the defender's shoulder position is the key. Any defender worth his salt will always try to shape up to the attacking player in a way that will dictate the attacking player's options. However, in doing so the defender will have two sides to his physical make up that could cause him defensive problems. He will be either weak or strong on one side of the body, depending on his body position/stance. Knowing this (see the shape of the defender's shoulders) information will help the attacking player (player A) to choose his playing options and to therefore work the ball against the defender more successfully.

Only In Practice - In the above simple example, the defender has played the ball to the attacking practice player A and has moved in on the ball. It is the attacking player's job to translate the defender's shoulder position into his evasive action. If the defender challenges for the ball with his left foot then the attacking player will move the ball to the right. In the above example, player A works on moving the ball off the line to the side of the defender's left shoulder and forward of that shoulder position.

From a playing point of view - The skill of moving the ball off the line can be performed -

1 - On the move
2 - From a static position
3 - Off a feint (sending the opponent the wrong way)

Slow or Fast Skills - There are some touch options that are performed to a slower, less sharp effect and others that can be very fast. Slow and fast skills can dictate the pace of the game, but so can the actions of the opponent. There are times when the opponent will make the choice of touch easier by his lack of thought when trying to win possession of the ball. The above cone placement example shows that more clearly. Here the player takes the slow touch option of moving the ball off the line with the inside instep of the left foot and plays the ball across the his body, as shown by the above example. Although this action does result in a slower physical movement, the result is still positive if the opponent has committed himself to the tackle. If the opponent lunges in with his left foot as shown above, the player in possession of the ball will move the ball against the challenging foot, which in this case is to his right. In general terms if the opponent tries to win the ball with the left foot then the attacking player uses the right foot to move the ball to the left. If, on other hand, the opponent tries to win the ball with the right foot then the attacking player will use the left foot to move the ball to the right.

Changing the pace of the game

The drag back of the ball as practiced in the straight line of cones is a faster skill than the inside instep across the body touch but the fastest skill still is the sweep of the underside of the boot across the top of the ball. The proper choice of skills and the way the player utilizes the skills in question is determined by the playing problems on the pitch. However, the choice of skill can in fact determine the pace of the game. For example -

1 - Passing the ball on the first contact with the ball
2 - Taking the slow or fast touch option
3 - Taking more than one touch
4 - Dribbling with the ball rather than passing
5 - Use combinations - Use a skill sequence, play the 1-2
6 - Pass the ball to feet/space

The resulting playing effects - 1 - Speeds the game up -2- Does both - 3- Slows the game down - 4- Slows the game down -5- Speeds the game up - 6 - Speeds the game up

ADVANCED FORMATS

Moving on - It is commonplace nowadays that at times during the game the player will have to keep possession of the ball against more than one opposing defender. The skill of keeping the ball against more than one defender lies in combining different touch options and working the ball to the correct angles. The following example deals with the problem of having to take on more than one challenger for the ball. When the attacking player has to deal with more than one opponent, he will have to combine the slow skills with the fast feet skills in order to keep possession of the ball. The skill of taking on the defenders head on is performed to the same angle as above but the sequence will involve the use of a combination of skills to do the job. When the area of play is reduced by the close proximity of the defenders, the attacking player needs to keep the ball close to his body, especially against the second defender. Dealing with the second challenger in most cases requires the use of the faster skills because in normal playing circumstances 'The second challenger' may leave the attacking player (having dealt with the first challenger) with very little time or space to move the ball out of the way.

Part 2 - The Missing Movement Elements

The following format enables the player to work on developing his fast skill options for moving the ball against the second challenger.

Fast Feet -

Here we are working not only on the fast feet required to do the job effectively but also the ability to apply the two quick touches off the forward touch combination that will effectively take on the second challenger. The skill of taking on more than one defender involves taking the off the line skill and combining that with a working movement combination called 'The Inverted Steps'.

The Skill Combination Format
Fast Feet 'Inverted Steps'

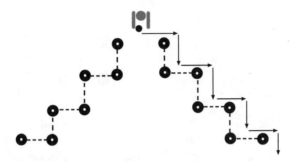

The Inverted Steps Skill - The first challenger is taken care of by applying the skill of moving the ball off the line. - The second challenger will be beaten by utilizing the skill combination that applies the lateral to forward short touch combination. The skill of dealing with the second challenger, therefore, is made up of two parts and the 'Inverted Steps Format' clearly shows what is involved. If you care to take a closer examination of the above diagram the practice of the movements can take place on the right and left side of the format. In order to develop the ability to move to the right or left of the defender the practice takes place to the right and left of the working format.

The Above Format - To achieve the objective of moving past the second defender, the cones are placed on the ground to form a shape that looks like steps/stairs. Can you see the shape? The best way to understanding the side to forward inside instep action with the ball when working the ball down this format would be to get the reader to try to imagine a ball rolling down a staircase. Look at the action from the side of the staircase and reverse the movements in your mind, instead of having the object roll down the stairs, imagine it rolling up the stairs. If you can do that then you can more or less observe the movements of the feet in the above format. In visual terms when the cones are placed on the ground to this 'steps shape' it is hard to spot the steps unless you know what to look for. To appreciate the shape I have drawn a line on paper from one cone to the next (cone to cone) to make the shape clearly visible to the reader. The short touch 'side to forward' combination option for working against the covering player stems from this format. So! The first challenger is taken care of by applying the 'off the line' skill, while the second challenger is dealt with by applying the movements learned in the 'Inverted Steps format'.

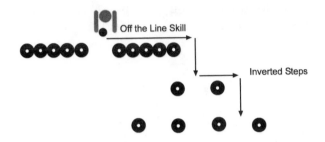

Note - The training formats are linked up to create the playing solution. In the above diagram I have simply linked the formats to show you the progressive attitude to training. All formats lead to the development of the ability to use the ball. The single line of cones underpins the 'Two cone placement and the 'Inverted Steps' format and so on. The inverted steps format is explained in detail later. The best way to practice is to practice first and foremost the individual skills involved separately and then bring the skills involved together as shown above to form the complete working sequence. This is shown in the following explanations.

Fast Feet - It stands to reason that if you can repeat a skill (individual skill) several times over you can improve on that skill in a number of ways. The inverted steps format is an example of a repetition that affords the player the opportunity to practice the fast physical development of the shorter and longer length of touch options. The combined practice benefit to the player of working out in this method of training is as follows -

(a) The player can learn to move the ball off the line
(b) The player can learn to play the short and longer length of the forward touch.
(c) The player can learn to combine the use of the skills in question
(d) The player can learn to create skill combinations based on the fundamental options
(e) The player can develop the strength and ability to move from a lateral position.
(f) The player can learn to use both feet
(g) The player can move the ball to any direction

It is clear from a practice point of view that each player should have access to working formats that enable him to practice as many playing solutions as possible. In any event, many of the above objectives can only be achieved by repetition. The development of the player's playing repertoire is achieved by positioning the cones to recreate the appropriate soccer movements, movements specific to any playing skill.

The Development Of Fast Feet

As I have said before, there are different ways of slowing or speeding up the game of soccer. The player can employ physical movements that either slow the game down or speed the game up. Whatever his choice of action, one thing is clear, if the player is not developed properly he will not be able to change the pace of his physical actions.

In addition to the above efforts the player needs to develop his ability to move his feet in such a way that he can implement the change in the pace of his work.

FAST FEET & SKILL COMBINATIONS

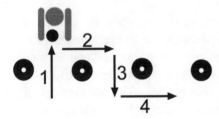

1 = The drag back with the underside of the right boot, this touch brings the ball back to the player's side of the cones.

2 = The right inside instep moving the ball to the player's left.

3 = Forward touch with left instep

4 = The sweep of the boot over the ball, taking the ball across the top of the format.

The Best Way Forward - The best way to develop fast feet is to work on this issue separately in specialized formats that focus entirely on the development of fast feet. We have already begun the development of the player's strength to use his feet because the quest to achieve this objective takes place in the straight line of cones. When working the ball within the single line of cones the working possibilities on the ball can be reflective of the fact that some skills are fast and others pose a physical problem and are, therefore, more difficult to perform quickly. The beginning of fast feet development comes from the differences between the skills in use, whether a skill is fast or slow promotes the development of the changes in the pace of work and those changes in turn develop the player's fast feet capability. Use the single line of cones to create any number of playing combinations. For example -

Begin - Foot on top of the ball - Sweep the ball with the underside of the right boot across (one gap only)

Next - Drag the ball back with the underside of the left boot and move the ball back to the player's side of the line.

Next - Move the ball with the inside instep of the right foot to the left (one gap only)

Next - Punch the ball through the line with the inside instep of the left foot.

Next - Play the sweep with the underside of the right boot and play the ball across the top of the line again and so on

Keep the sequence going to the end of the line of cones. Remember to work the ball to the left and right of the format.

Note - When you are working with a number of players, use a rotational solution to get the players moving in and through the format. When a player comes to the end of the line of cones with the ball and finishes his working sequence on the ball he will then take a forward touch to the ball and move the ball out of the line of cones. The forward touch at the end of the working sequence takes place with the left foot on the left side of the format and the right foot on the right of the format.

Variations - The skill sequence can be altered to include any combination you like. For example - Keep to the above skills but instead of sweeping the ball across one gap, move the ball over two gaps.

Fast feet - Good Feet - call it what you will. One thing is for certain, the ability to move the feet quickly can be developed only by the application of specialized formats. If the player is encouraged to be strong only on one side of the body, his weak leg will not be able to move as fast to the ball. Defenders pose different problems for the attacking player and therefore there are different solutions that need to be applied. Most answers require the lateral format solutions.

The working composition

There would be little point to the formats if at the end of the day the end product created zero effect. The following working formats create playing effects that enable the player to deal with opponents who are trying to retain possession of the ball. The player in possession of the ball, on other hand, does his best to keep the ball and to create a playing effect that has an end product. The end product could be anything from passing the ball to a strike on goal. In this next example, the skill format looks at helping the player develop a way of hiding his playing intentions.

Fast Feet Skills - The Double Bluff Skill

The following analogy explains the core movements of the double bluff. Imagine the player playing the ball from one gap to the next with the inside instep of either foot very quickly, but not actually moving to any direction. The art of disguising your intentions and sending the wrong playing message to your opponent can be based on this simple action example. There are different ways of disguising the playing intention. One of them we already mentioned (dropping the shoulder), another could be playing the ball unexpectedly with the outside of the boot and so on. Sending the wrong message effectively requires skill, in particular fast feet skill.

Developing the strength side of the equation - The first thing to do was in fact to develop the inside instep movements with the ball.

The fast feet development part of training will take place in a realistic setting. In other words, the work on fast feet will take place in conjunction with the development of a soccer playing skill. Everything has a starting point and the birth of the double bluff skills is no different. Remember the action in the single line of cones. The ball is moved

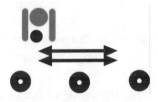

The 'Double Bluff'

from one inside instep to the next down the line of cones. Look at the above three cone placement. The two lateral arrows show the player moving the ball on the spot without going anywhere, moving the ball from one inside instep to the next four times. Take the cones away and imagine the player doing exactly the same on the spot, moving the ball from one inside instep to the next. This is the basic movement of the double bluff skill.

Why Bother With Cones?

If you can do the above movements without the cones, why bother with the cones? One serious reason is the development of the player's ability to stay square on to the action and another is the development of the player's ability to move in a consistent way. A consistent working pattern is crucial in the development of the skills in question. The most important of all player attributes when taking on any opponent has to be the ability to disguise his intentions. This is closely followed by the player's ability to move quickly and precisely. The ability to do so comes from having fast feet and excellent coordination. For all those reasons it is vital to appreciate the importance of the practice of moving the ball with the inside instep down the line of cones and the resulting ability to keep 'square on' to the movements in order to be able to move in any direction. The development of fast feet for the playing of the 'Double bluff' skill takes place to the following sequence -

The Working principles - A double or triple bank of arrows (or more) represents the fast movements of the ball from one inside instep of the foot to the next, in rapid succession. The number of touches on the ball can vary, depending on the player's decision when to move the ball away. The fast inside instep movements with the ball constitute 'The bluff' part of the skill. The fast feet keep the ball in place but which way will the player move with the ball? It is impossible for the defender to know which direction the attacking player will go next.

When moving the ball to the right of the format, the player leads the movements with the inside instep of the left foot. When moving the ball out to the left of the format, he leads the movements with the inside instep of the right foot.

The Touch - Touch - Move

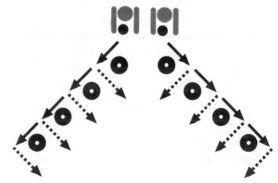

The 'Touch Touch & Move' - On the left, the left foot inside instep moves the ball to the angle and gaps shown and on the right it is the right foot inside instep that moves the ball to the player's left.

Instructions - Take a look at the above shape and angle of the cone placements. The solid arrows show the inside instep short touch options taken to the ball to the 'set up' angle by the attacking player. The touch options to this angle are numbered 1 to 4 on the left and right of the format. The dashed arrows represent the forward touch to lose the defender. The effectiveness of this touch depends on the number of dummy touches taken to this angle (is it 1,2 3, or 4 or more?)

THE BLUFF - The key to success, therefore, is based on keeping the defender moving and responding to the directional touch. If the defender responds to the direction of the attacking player's touch and moves in that direction then the attacking player should be able to choose that moment to move and lose his opponent. You should appreciate that player A can lose the defender on the first, second, third touch and so on. The practice sequence should therefore reflect on that possibility.

Note - It is possible to position a defender to the one side (the defensive side - away from the attacking player) to create a way of working that would help the attacking player practice moving the ball on the touch. The fact that I have no opponents in many of the working formats is of little consequence. This is in fact deliberately the case at times because it is my intention to develop soccer skills first and foremost and then let the player apply the skills learned during actual play or on the practice ground in special possession practice sessions. The application of the skills in question takes time and you will have to be patient when it comes to seeing the results of your endeavors. Always encourage the players to apply the skills in games of soccer but remember that many of the skills in question will only come through effectively when the player is strong enough to work the ball.

The Skill Definition

In the above format, moving the ball to the gaps numbered 1 to 4 can be called the 'Bluff touch' while moving the ball to the dashed arrow direction can be called the 'Evasive touch'. As seen above, the 'Bluff touch' can be performed with the right inside instep or the left inside instep or with the sweep action of the underside of the boot. Moving the ball explosively away, the 'Evasive touch', can be performed with the outside of the boot or the inside instep or again the sweep technique. In all events the inside instep touches are performed from a 'square on' body position and the final length of touch is reflective of the player's needs in terms of the action taken.

Strength Development - The ability to move to any direction counters the tactical instruction of the jockeying principles - The instructions put to the **DEFENDER** to position the attacking player onto his so-called bad side would in fact stand bankrupt.

Explanation - When the defender gives way (backs off) the touches taken to the ball are angled in response to the defender's movements. The body, though, must stay 'Square On' to the action. If the attacking player did not stay 'Square on' to the action he would make the defender's job easier and the ability to change the direction of the action would be difficult.

Remember that it is possible to lose the defender on any of the touch options shown here. It is therefore essential to reflect that in practical terms. It is possible to play the ball with the outside of the boot or even take a double buff action and move off with the ball.

The Practical Change Of Direction Options - For developing fast feet and quick changes in direction, the player can begin from any point in the working line. This depends on how fast you want the player to move out of the format or how many touches you want the player to work with. The practice sequence can take place from a standing position at any point in the format or from a moving position outside of the format. Every player can begin to work the format from a pass, taking control of the ball and then moving the ball to the format at position 1, 2 , 3 or 4 . The work is simply undertaken with the inside instep of the right or left foot and the escape with the ball can be imaginative.

The Touch Sequence - This can be anything you want - The starting position in the line would obviously reflect on the skill combination possibility - For example: Move the ball with - The Inside instep - 3, 4 & out = Touch, touch, move and play; The inside instep - 4 & out = Touch, move and play; The inside instep - 2, 3, 4 & out = Touch, touch, touch move and play; The inside instep - 4 & out Touch = Touch, move and play (use outside of the boot).

Back To 'The Double Bluff'

I have introduced the 'one off' format and angle here and the touch options available because it is possible to combine the skills in question to form a playing solution. It is incredible what the player can do with the simple inside instep playing technique. Once again the basis for the following combination option comes from the original movements practiced in the straight line of cones, the basic 'sideways on' inside instep movements. The following example is once again all about developing fast feet for the double bluff and the lateral ability to move the ball rapidly away from any defender. The angle of work is once again lateral and the playing option can be said to be standard. In this next example, we will take a look at how to develop the player's ability to actually move the ball to the right or left of the defender.

The Technical Make Up of the Format

The definition of the second part of the double bluff skill can be called 'The 'Tap Tap'. The name comes from the sound made when moving the ball from one inside instep to the next, in quick succession. The illustration shows the cone placements that enable the player to begin the working sequence with the ball that creates the double bluff playing action. Placing the cones wider than shoul-

der width enables the player to practice moving the ball with the inside instep 'tap tap' action (performed with the inside instep of the right and left foot) through the gate. The reasons for working through the gate to this movement pattern is as follows -

1 - To keep the player upright
2 - To keep the ball in a playable position
3 - To keep the feet moving

Moving the ball through the gap forces the player to work from an upright and therefore square on body position. This forms the basis for the first part of this combination skill action - also known as 'The Tap Taps and Move'.

Next -Develop the ability to play the ball off the bluff action. Escaping with the ball at an appropriate moment 'off' the tap taps movements is a matter of timing. When the player does move the ball off the line, he must do it explosively, to the right or left of the defender at the point when the defender tries to win the ball.

The 'Bluff & Move' Format

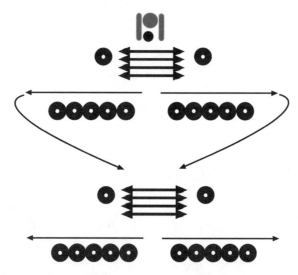

Points of reference - Once the player is through the narrow gate he moves the ball explosively (left or right) with an off the line touch. In this example, I have shown only two narrow gate placements and two off the line cone placements (evasive touch placements), but it is possible to have as many as five each.

The Double Bluff Skill Is Born -

Sometime during the fast feet inside instep movements through the gate, player A takes an evasive 'off the line' touch to the ball. Linking the two separate skills in this way forms the double bluff. Moving the ball to the side off the short inside instep movements should be done in an explosive manner. Such an action surprises the opponent and sends him the wrong way.

The reason for the shape - The set up of the narrow and wide gates makes the format interesting. When the player moves through the narrow gate his body position is ideal for moving both himself and the ball to the side and therefore to the correct working position for the second part of the equation. The second part uses the 'off the line' touch. This side movement taken with the inside instep of the appropriate foot takes the ball away from the challenger. The ability to link up the bluff and the 'off the line' skill creates a very effective way of getting away from the opposing player.

Technique & Strength

As I have already said, it is important to support the skills development (working with the ball) with measures that effectively strengthen the player's physical ability to play the skills in question. The secret lies in targeting specific movements in a repetitive manner.

On the Move

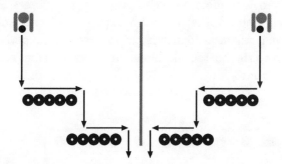

For Attacking Play -

The above cone placement helps to develop the skill of moving the ball off the line on the move against the first and second challenger for the ball. Essentially, the development of some skill options takes place in many different training environments for the simple reason that the application of some soccer playing skills also takes place in different ways. The playing of a skill could take place on the move, on the ground, in the air, in competition with opponents, in free space and so on. One of the most difficult things to do on the move (when running with the ball) is to play any skill to a movement pattern that's perfect for that skill. Perfection is something that is almost impossible, but achieving a good working skill definition is not. The length and distance of any cone placement on the ground in front of player A (the five cones that form the lateral line) facilitate the correct practice pattern for performing the evasive movements against any challenging player. The working distance from one set of cones to the next is 1 yard.

Note - In the above format the work includes the practice of taking up a long pass (from the last player in), the forward touch and the touch that moves the ball off the line to the next working shape.

Moving 'Inside Or Outside' With the Ball

The ability to switch play and, therefore, to play the game to any direction can only be done effectively by players who possess the ability to use the right or left foot.

The Main Points Of Reference - The players should be able to work the ball to any direction. If the coaching of players is limited to the pass and move conditioned game of soccer, the players' playing repertoire will simply not enable them to play to a higher standard. The raising of playing standards depends on practice and on paying meticulous attention to the correct development of movements related to soccer play options.

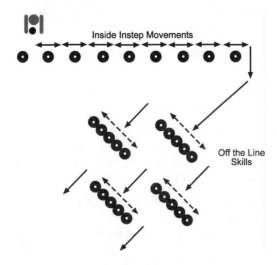

Once you have the information and the code for the working formats you can create effective advanced movement formats that enable the player to work on any objective you like. It is very simple to bring together the different elements and provide the player with a working format that will help him to develop his physical capability to move with the ball. It is a question of understanding the function of the lateral movements and the shapes or cone placements. When it comes to the layout of the format, you must take into consideration the realities of the game. Picture, for example, the first challenger putting pressure on the player in possession of the ball. If he has assistance, where would that assistance come from? In other words, the position of the opposition is taken into account as well as the skills that will be used to solve the playing problems. The practice formats, therefore, are positioned in a way that reflects the playing action.

Note - The above example will provide the player with excellent short touch options and moving the ball off the line combinations. It can easily be said that the objective of the working formats is to raise the level of the player's effort on the ball. To understand the connection between all the working formats thus far, simply go back to the examples given or see the working code at the end of the book.

Developing the First Touch

All lateral forms of training can be said to be fundamental to the development of the first touch. That being said, it is impossible to learn the 'first touch' on the ball options without the use of specialized working formats. The development of the first touch utilizes cone placement formats that create the correct dimensions for the development of the ability to play the first touch to almost any direction. Everyone recognizes a quality player by his ability to take a first touch on the ball. A quality player is not an accident of nature. Quality players are not defined by opinion, but by the way they can use the ball and therefore define the quality of touch. As far as the working formats go it is the job of the cone placements to help the player achieve his playing excellence in terms of the first touch.

The Standard First Touch Options - The design of the cone placements recognizes the existence of certain technical playing objectives. For example, the ability of the player to move in a way that will enable him to see other playing options early.

The Practice Of The 'First Touch' Options

The Two-Cone Placement - First of all please allow me to explain the reason for some of the measurements and distances involved in the first of my examples on the development of the first touch. Once again, the 'Single line of cones' underpins the development of the first touch because in that format the player works on developing his feel for the ball and more importantly his inner groin strength to play the ball effectively. Subsequently, the two-cone placement is fundamental to this work. The following cone placement examples formulate the correct dimensions for the development of the basic first touch skills. The significance of the two-cone placement lies in the technical aspects of training. First and foremost, the distance between the two cones and the position of the practicing player forms a special relationship. This relationship forms the correct angles for the practice of the 'Set Up Touch' and the touch that moves the ball 'off the line'. If you did not have the two-cone placement practice format and the following working formats, you could not possibly achieve the practice objective of developing the skills correctly. This is simply because in order to practice the proper first touch, the practice of the skills in question has to adhere to a specific sequence of movements. The number one objective is to define the movements involved. Next, we must provide the player a guideline that enables him to work on the skills in question to a consistent working pattern. In effect we are talking about a repetition format that establishes the correct foot position to the ball and the body position in relation to the direction of touch, together with the correct weight and angle of touch. The most important principles of skill development are-

1 - The Quality Of The Practice
2 - The Consistency 'Of' The Practice Endeavors

In addition to the main principles there is also the small matter of developing the player's ability to look up when in possession of the ball. That ability requires special training because it is simply not natural to look up when concentrating on the ball. The two-cone placement, for example, takes into account the implications of the first touch when considering what touch to use (see 1 to 4). The two-cone placement, therefore, is used to begin the development of the standard playing sequence. The work in these formats adheres to the following physical and technical playing endeavors:

1 - Head Up - Look up prior to receiving the ball to assess the options
2 - Head Down - Look down on the ball 'Take a touch' & Look up
3 - Look Down - Implement the playing option
4 - Look up - Reassess the playing position and support the play

Developing Good Habits - The first touch development cone placements deliver the proper working environment for achieving the above objectives in a practical manner. In addition to that it is also important for the player to be able to play the ball to any direction on the first touch. For that reason, the development of the first touch must take place in a practice format that reflects on all possibilities available to the player. There are progressive cone placements that will do that job effectively. The 'Three - Cone placement', for example, is there to enable the player to move on from the 'square on' body position and achieve the ability to play the ball from a ¼ turned body position as well so that he can bridge the work between the   'two - cone placement' with other formats such as the 'four cone placement'. Together, these form the main working environment that enables the player to develop his ability to play his first touch in any direction.

The Complete Set of Standard First Touch Options

1 - The Set Up' Touch (inside instep)
2 - The Change of Angle Touch (inside instep)
3 - The Forward Touch (inside instep)
4 - The Reverse Touch (inside instep)
5 - The Change of Angle with Depth Touch (inside instep)
6 - The Dink Touch (toe down laces)
7 - The Roll Touch (outside of the foot)

Their Function On 'The Soccer Pitch'- The seven touch options listed above enable the player to play the ball to a 360° angle.

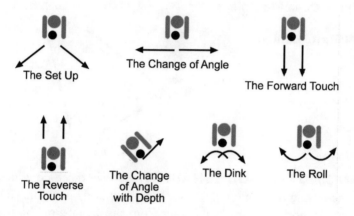

Technical Considerations - The body is able to move the ball and the player 180° to the left and 180° to the right. The ability to play to any direction depends on the above body and foot position to the ball and of-course the correct choice of skill. The choice of action is supported by choosing the correct first touch option. There is absolutely everything wrong with the player who takes the ball up on his left side when the ball is clearly positioned to his right. Any player (right footed or left footed) who has to adjust his body position to take up the ball has playing limitations. Quality players are able to take the ball up as it comes to them, maximizing their options on the next touch.

The Definition of the Direction of Play Possibilities

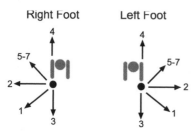

Right Foot   Left Foot

This represents the playing capability of 180° to the left and right of the player. The skills numbered 1 to 7 are the first touch options available to the player.

The Development Of The Skills In Question

**The Three Cone Placement
and
the 1/4 Turn Position**

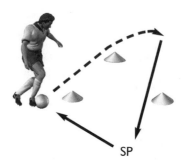

SP

CHANGING THE BODY SHAPE - The above three-cone placement shows the touch played from a ¼ turned body position. The reason that this body position is different from the 'Square on' body position is that it represents the half -way point in the 180 degree turn
between the square on position (facing the pass) and the complete
turn of the body in terms of playing all the first touch options. In the
following body position examples, the dotted lines show the ball coming to the player from (SP). On playing the appropriate touch the player
adapts his body position to the ball and takes it up with the appropriate foot position, moving the foot on the touch to the direction of the
touch.

Interactive Formats - In addition to the development of the first
touch, we also need to take a look at the practice formats that involve
passing the ball and interactive play. To do that the cone placements
take on a different shape. In addition to the four cone placement, there
is a need to employ additional cones to the outside in order to facilitate other playing options. This will not only develop the ability to play
off the first touch, but will involve the practice of passing the ball off a
sequence of movements.

First things first - Learning to move 'off the first touch' to any direction is the number one priority. Playing the first touch effectively makes all the difference to the player's game because a quality touch on the ball will enable him to:

1 - make the time to play the next option
2 - make room to play the next option
3 - open up different angles of play
4 - position the ball to a (better) playable angle
5 - improve his control of what takes place - 'quality of touch'
6 - improve the quality of the team performance

The Four - Cone Placement
Directional Options of the First Touch

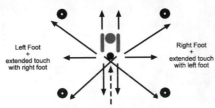

Left Foot
+
extended touch
with right foot

Right Foot
+
extended touch
with left foot

Average length of touch = 1.5 yds

The four-cone placement enables the player to complete the practice of all the basic first touch options (1 to 7). The working position is of course 'The Square On Body Position' and the complete turn is performed by applying the number 4 skill option which is known as the 'Reverse touch'. This touch completes the body rotation from the face on position (Square On) to the complete turn around (back to service). The above diagram shows the complete range of basic first touch options that allow the player to move the ball 180 degrees to either the left or right. The complete set of first touch options makes it possible for the player to work the ball to a total of 360° 'off' the first touch.

Why bother? - When the player is able to define his first touch options to a meaningful direction he will be in greater control of his game. Obviously, when we consider the speed of the game and the limited space and time that players are allowed, a skillful and purposeful first touch is an absolute requirement. A player with no idea of the first touch options available will always be a liability. Also, it is always better to move the ball in an economical way because it will save energy. It should be obvious that through the development of standard first touch options it is possible to enable the player to take better control of his game.

Playing Solutions

In some ways the touch angle dictates the working format. The following example of the use of the 'Forward Touch' (angle option 3) can be worked on in the 'Four - Cone' Placement Format.

The Playing Problem - When the defender is very close to the back of the player in possession. The 'forward touch' as shown in the four cone placement gives the solution - In this example the player works the ball away from the defender with the inside instep of the right foot. This touch will enable the attacking player to keep the ball and play his way out of trouble.

The practical points of the practice - The service of the ball by SP to the practicing player is to the appropriate foot. For practical reasons, SP plays the ball to the right inside instep or the left inside instep - Player A moves the ball on the first touch straight ahead with the inside instep of the right or left foot.

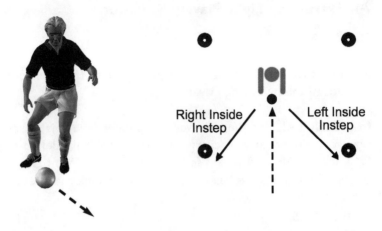

Practice 'The Set Up Touch' - SP plays the ball to player A - Player A uses the inside instep of the right or left foot to play the ball to the angles shown by the arrows. Option 1 = Player A plays the ball with the inside instep of his left foot to his right (to the angle shown) and his right foot playing the ball to his left again to the angle shown. This movement represents the first touch option called 'The Set Up Touch'. The set up touch is made in anticipation of the next touch. Skill option number 1 can also be utilized when the player wants to strike the ball. When practicing, keep square on to the touch, move the foot in the direction of the touch, move on the touch and knock the ball back to the service player.

An Extremely Tight Playing Situation

MAN ON

For Dink Touch Options - SP plays the ball to the right foot or the left foot of the practicing player.

In practice - Lifting the ball over an opponent's foot is a useful skill against an opponent who charges in for the ball. In order to play the Dink Touch - Player A moves forward towards the front two cones in the format and lifts the ball from SP using the dink touch over the appropriate cone.

Playing the Dink Touch - As the ball arrives to the player's foot, he points his toe down and puts the laces under the ball, lifting his foot on contact with the ball to send it over the cone (defender's foot). Which foot should the player dink the ball with? If the opponent lunges in with his right foot, the attacker should use his left and vice versa.

Improvisation - There is nothing wrong with using some imagination. I use the practice of the 'Dink touch' as a platform for the creation of an imaginative skills sequence. 'The Dink Touch' can start a working sequence that can be made up of the following movements with the ball - 1 - The player could 'Dink' the ball (use play option 6) with the right foot to send the ball in the air, on the bounce the player can then flick the ball back the other way using the outside of the same foot, when the ball lands again he uses the inside instep of the left foot to start a double bluff move to set up the pass back to SP.

TO OPEN UP THE ANGLE OF PLAY
The Extended Touch

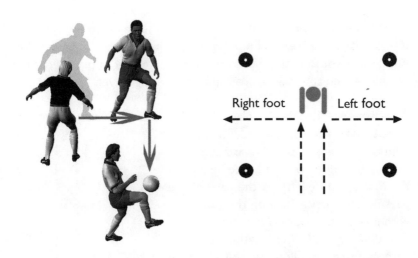

Right foot   Left foot

Moving the ball off the line - The skill of moving the ball off the line has two functions - To open up areas of play for different playing options and to keep possession of the ball. This important touch can be performed in two ways -

Play the ball across the body

Extend the foot away from the body

In Skill option 1 -The foot follows the ball, thus becoming the first stride in the direction of the touch. Moving the ball across the body with the inside instep is not the quickest option, but it has its uses. **Skill option 2** to the same angle is the quicker move. The player simply extends his foot to a 90° angle, playing the ball with the outside of the foot or the instep and moving in the direction of the touch. Playing off the first touch is therefore crucial to the ability of playing the ball on the second touch away from the challenging player.

The Reverse Touch - SP plays the ball to the practicing player's right or left foot - The reverse touch is of course opposite to the forward touch. Taking the ball up on the inside instep of the foot (right or left), let the pace of the pass do the work - Turn on the touch by withdrawing the foot on contact with the ball, allowing the ball to continue on its path, and turn to follow the ball. Make sure the defender is on the side away from the touch.

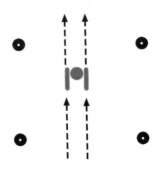

The Reverse Touch

Let the pace of the pass do the work.

The Roll Touch - Skill option 7 - Similar to the dink touch - The dink touch is played across the body - The roll touch is played outward away from the body. SP plays the ball to the outside of the player's left or right foot. The receiver flicks the ball around the corner of the defender with the outside of the boot (toe pointing down). He then spins around the defender on that touch, turning the ball around the corner of the defender. This 'Roll touch' skill is utilized when the opponent is marking 'tight on' behind the attacking player. Use this skill to 'Spin off' the defender.

Handy Hints
Moving On The Touch

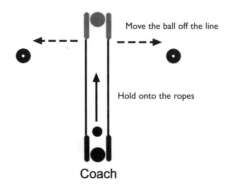

Move the ball off the line

Hold onto the ropes

Coach

'Keeping Square On' - The most difficult thing for any young player to do is to keep his shoulders still and 'square on' to the action while moving his body (right or left) on the touch. This is because most young players are (at the outset of their physical development) weak on one side of the body. What can help the young player at the outset to gain a better physical understanding of the 'square on body' position on the touch is to apply the above example. In difficult cases get a long elastic rope and ask the player to hold one end in each hand. The 'Coach' in turn holds on to the elastic rope at the opposite end. By holding on to the elastic rope 'The Coach' can hold the player face on (square on) to the action while the player moves his body 'square on' to the left or right.

How Does This Help?
The proper way to move the ball on the first touch is to employ a follow through on the touch. When working on the 'Set Up Touch' in the two cone placement, for example, that means the foot moves across the body and to the direction of the touch. In the event of passing the ball on the second touch, the follow through ensures the start of a specific working sequence. The working sequence is defined as 'The touch, move and play' sequence. Getting the player to make the connection between the square on body position and the sequence of touch, move and play in this way may solve the player's understanding of how to move on the touch correctly. Once this has been achieved the player has the foundation for working on different first touch options because the principle of the movements involved apply to all the fundamental first touch options.

Dealing With Player Numbers - The working formats are not restrictive in terms of the number of players that can be accommodated. The simplest way to take care of the numbers of players involved is to position two or three formats on the practice ground or to split the players into groups of four or five. It is then quite easy to spend ten to fifteen minutes on each format, with players moving from format to format. There are different ways of working the formats:

1 - The players can work on improving a single playing skill.
2 - The players can work on linking up different skills.
3 - The players can rotate to a working sequence.
4 - The players can work in twos (learn to be a team player)

Moving the foot correctly

If the player finds it difficult to move the foot across his 'Square on' body position to the direction of the touch, place two cones at the center of the main 'Two - Cone Placement' to help him with this problem. Place the cones in the center but not in the way of the movements with the ball. When the cones are in place as shown, ask the player to make sure that on contact with the ball his foot moves past the two small cones at the center of the format before the rest of his body.

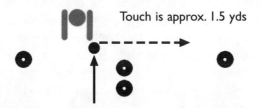

Touch is approx. 1.5 yds

When the player works in the above cone placement on the skill of moving the ball off the line with or without the center guidelines, the service of the ball has to be played to the correct foot position. If the player is working on moving the ball off the line to his left (when facing the service player) then the service player must play the ball to the inside instep of the right foot. The exception to this rule is when the player applies the extended foot touch on the ball to the direction of the touch. If the player is moving the ball to his right, facing the service player, then the service player must play the ball to the left foot.

Dealing with Numbers - The Two-Cone Rotational Format -

With a large number of players, some skills can be isolated and worked on in a conveyer type manner.

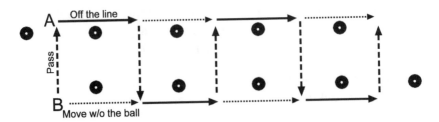

The Conveyor Belt System

In the above example I have created a single format that caters to moving the ball off the line, working in twos. This shape is designed to enable both players to work the ball off the line on the move. To practice moving the ball off the line each player moves the ball on his designated side of the format as shown by the lateral arrows and with his second touch passes the ball to the other player who moves the ball off the line with his first touch and so on. At the end of the sequence, the players can play one-twos back to the starting position.

Good ball control skills and accuracy of passing - It is of course important that when the players work the ball off the line in this way that they keep to the working principles of moving the foot on the touch. This will help the players to move the ball correctly and to be on time to receive the next pass up the line. Players can swap sides on completion of a working sequence. The player at the top of the format will move the ball to his left with the inside instep of the right foot while at the bottom side of the format the player will move the ball to his right with the inside instep of his left foot. As you can see, it is quite easy to cater to large numbers of players by using this rotational system (conveyer belt).

Alternatively - It is possible to have the two players working the ball to the end of the format and back, two or three times before letting the next working pair in. It's a question of how much time you have to work with your players or how many players you are working with as to which option you will take. If you have lots of players to work with then ultimately the best solution may lie in creating more than one working shape.

Dealing with numbers - Moving the ball off the line in depth in numbers in a three - cone placement is achieved in this next example of a conveyor system. To get the correct effect or angle of the movements required to move the ball off the line with depth, place the cones on the ground to form a figure (S) Shape. Working the ball to the bend in the shape forces the player to move the ball to the correct angle.

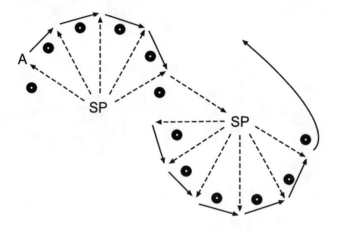

USING THE BODY

If you have ever played golf you know that the golf shot is dependent on a number of physical attributes. Some of the physical attributes focus on the player's ability to use his legs and shoulders (upper body) correctly when performing the golf swing. When it comes to playing soccer (or any other sport for that matter) the problem of using the body correctly in relation to the skill you are performing is in many ways the same. There are common features among every sporting endeavor that come to the forefront and the ability to move the body properly is certainly a feature that links all sporting activities. Whether making a golf swing or kicking the ball, the technique is dependent on the physical ability to position the body correctly.

Learning To Shape Up - It is vital to teach players to appreciate the use of the body when playing different soccer skills. The practical work on the first touch options has certainly done that but in addition we need to enable the player to practice re - positioning his body quickly in order to change the playing solution. The following format is designed to teach the player the difference between the square on body position and the ¼ turned body position. The quality of the player's performance is based on the way he shapes his body to the ball. This makes all the difference to the quality and choice of the technique. In the following format the player will also practice getting his body behind the ball early on in the working sequence. This is especially important to the player when he receives the ball or makes the pass.

Square On   1/4 Turned Right   1/4 Turned Left   Square On

Using The Body - Shape Up - Player A moves his body from 'The square on body position' to the ¼ turn body position (to the left and right). The working sequence begins and ends with the 'Square on' body position.

The Practice Format

During the following practice sequence player A will apply the 'Square On' body position that will enable him to play the simple lateral 'off the line touch' and the ¼ turned body position that will enable him to play the 'off the line touch' with depth. The angled touches are played to the player's right and or left side in the three - cone placement format. The following is a touch, pass and move working sequence that naturally involves the use of the pass.

The Composition 'Of' 'The Working Format' - The practice format is made up of the 'Two & Three Cone Placement Formats'

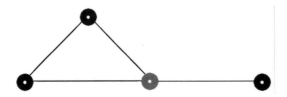

The two and three cone formats are joined together to form a single format. It is possible to make the area smaller so that the younger players can work the ball and make the pass more easily. The dimensions can be reduced from 2 yds to 1.5 yds. The length of pass can also be determined by the distance between the cones at either end.

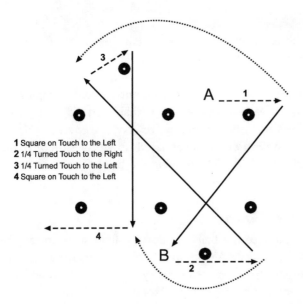

1 Square on Touch to the Left
2 1/4 Turned Touch to the Right
3 1/4 Turned Touch to the Left
4 Square on Touch to the Left

The Theme Of 'The Practice' - The point of the practice is to develop the ability to move the body 'off' the touch or the pass. This is the theme of the practice. Moving 'off' on the touch puts the player in the right place at the right time to receive or pass the ball on.

The Practice Guidelines Sequence - I - Player A begins the practice sequence by playing the ball to the lateral angle. Player A plays the ball to player B - Player B takes up the pass with the left inside instep and moves the ball 'off the line' at an angle to the right, as shown. Player B then makes a diagonal pass to player A who, after his original pass to Player B, has re-positioned in the three - cone part of the format. Player A has changed his body position from the square on to the ¼ turned. Player A moves the ball 'off the line' (angled again) to his left, to position 5, and plays a pass to player B who should now be in position 6. As the ball travels to player B from player A, Player A re-adjusts his body position and places himself to the other side of the three - cone placement format. The return pass from player B is made to the left side of the format to the inside instep of the player A's left foot. Player A moves the ball off the line again and passes the ball diagonally across the format to player B who now should be in position back on the other side of the format. The duration of the practice is left up to the Coach's discretion.

Confused?

If that's the case then all you have to do is to work out the movements according to the cone placement position. The square on body shape is applied in the two - cone placement and the quarter body turn position is applied in the three - cone placement twice. To simplify the movements all you have to remember is that each player on his side of the format moves from the square on to the ¼ turned position. In practice the touch with depth is repeated on either side of the three - cone placement and the skill of moving the ball 'off the line' is played once before the player moves on.

'Reading The Game'

Shaping up the body to the ball is important from a technical point of view but so is the ability to look up and to learn to read the game. The following example shows how to teach your players to read the game and to implement the correct playing solutions. The four - cone placement has four fundamental playing directions for the player to work to. The resulting working format will enable the player to practice how to make decisions quickly and what touch options to utilize in that decision making process. Every player should appreciate that the actual craft of keeping possession of the ball depends on taking stock of the whereabouts of the other players on the field (teammates and opponents) and the ability to read the game. In view of that fact it is important to teach the player how to use his playing options in relation to the teammates and opposing players around him. When using the four - cone placement as a foundation we can work on any number of playing solutions -

Appreciating Space - The following format enables the player to put into practice the first touch options in a game-like setting. In this next example the player learns to read the space around him and to implement the correct solution.

The Four Major Directional Playing Options Format

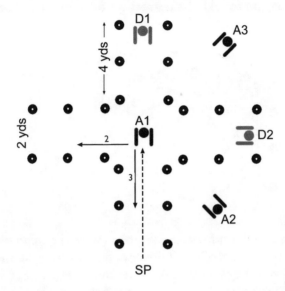

Working The Touch Options - The four - cone format is now used to establish a practical base for working on the player's ability to use the playing space around him effectively. The player will obviously use the playing solutions that involve the use of the fundamental first touch options. The above working channels, therefore, represent the first touch options available to the player that enable him to utilize the four major escape routes with the ball. The directional skills used here are -

Touch Options - 1 - The Forward Touch - The forward touch can be played with the right or left inside instep. 2 - The skill of moving the ball 'Off The Line' - Played with the inside instep of the right or left foot - This touch option can also be played with the inside instep taking the ball across the body or by applying 'The Extended Foot' touch to the ball. The 4th touch option used in this format is 'The Reverse Touch' - Played with the right or left inside instep.

The Practice Principles - In the above format the channels are used to create different playing problems. The creation of different playing problems is based on the positioning of the defensive and attacking players. The defensive players are positioned in the channels (not all channels are used) to the right or left of player A or to the back and/or front of player A. In addition to that, there are defensive and attacking players positioned to the outside of the format. The job of the practicing player at the center of the format is to see where the opponents have been placed and to take the correct action in order to keep the ball.

Example 1

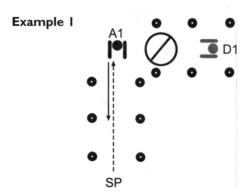

Choosing the touch and escape route - When the opponent is placed in the channel to the left of player A, player A can use the escape channel in front of him. If the player chooses to escape with the ball to this channel he would use the 'The forward touch' - The choice of which foot to use could also come into play. R= The right inside instep option. L = The left inside instep option.

Here, SP plays the ball to the player's right foot. The forward touch is used to get away from a defender who is marking the player tight or in order to get away from a defender that could affect possession. In the above example of the channel format player A has played the 'forward touch' with the inside instep of the right foot to get away from the defender positioned to his left.

Example 2

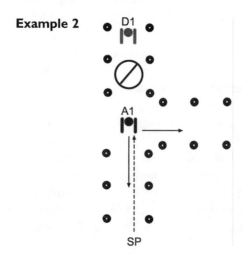

Playing option 2 - If the defender is positioned behind player A as shown example 2, the solution takes place to the front or side of player A in the format. The skill in use is the inside instep of the left foot taking the extended touch or the inside instep forward touch.

Note - Every player should be able to play the ball with the left or right foot. In any system of play, the players who are most effective are those who are able to play the ball to the above major directional play options. Once the player knows his playing options it is then relatively easy to teach him how to read the game. In every respect player A needs only to assess the position of the defensive player/s and make his choice of actions a reality. The above format represents the first touch escape routes. In other words, if you look at any playing system the position on the soccer pitch of any player lends itself to the above playing solutions.

In Practice - The practice sequence may be completed when the attacking player (the player in possession of the ball) is able to keep the ball (with his own teammates) in a designated area, for four consecutive passes. After the completion of the set task of four consecutive passes, all players can change their practice roles. The position of the attacking players and the defending players can be altered on each service of the ball. If you want to make things more difficult for the player taking the touch at the center of the format, ask the player to close his eyes for a moment. When the player has his eyes closed, re-locate the defenders (simply change the original defensive positions in the channels). The practicing player is then asked to open his eyes again and check the whereabouts of the defenders. The job of the practicing player is to assess the whereabouts of the opponents very quickly and deal with the ball that arrives at his feet. The first touch on the ball needs to take the ball to any channel that is free of opponents.

Defensively - The defenders come into play once the first touch is taken by player A. The defender's job is to stop the players in possession of the ball from achieving their objectives. It is also possible to put pressure on the player receiving the ball by allowing the defenders to move in closer to the center point of the format.

Taking Turns - Remember that some directional touch options can be played in two ways with the same foot. With this in mind, each player can stay at the center of the practice format until he has completed the full set of touch options available.

The Service - To Player A1 - It is important for any player to be able to read the game prior to making the pass. The position of the defenders (D1 & D2) in the format shows which side and to which foot the pass should be made when playing the ball to player A1. If player A1 is to have the best chance of retaining possession of the ball against the defenders, the pass will have to be made to the foot that's furthest away from any opponent. If the pass is made with such considerations in mind the player will be better able to select the correct playing option against the defensive positions and buy more time on the ball to carry out his playing intentions.

The Practical Reality - For more advanced players I would not exclude the practice of taking a confrontational touch in relation to any defender (See next chapter). A confrontational touch is one that places the player in possession of the ball directly into conflict with a defensive player. Keep in mind that the pace of the game can be altered depending on the touch taken. In the above examples, the defenders could be positioned closer to the practicing player.

Making The Right Playing Choice

Not all touch options have the same effect. I have already stated that not all touch options are fast and not all touch options are confrontational. By confrontational I mean attack minded. There are defensive touches on the ball that are designed to protect the ball and there are touches on the ball that are constructive touches that create more than one playing solution. The first touch, therefore, can be applied for different reasons. There are negative reasons and there are positive reasons for taking a touch to the ball. One of the more constructive reasons for the first touch is to surprise your opponent by confronting him head on, for example.

Which Touch? - The positive or the negative? - There are safe touch options and there are confrontational touch options. The decision of what touch to use can be based on the player's assessment of the following facts:

1 - What is the distance between the player in possession of the ball and the nearest defender. How much time does the player have to play the ball?

2 - What are the playing options?

3 - What type of skills does the player possess?

Such questions are answered by the practice formats. The cone placements represent the position of the defenders and therefore the practice area for working on escape routes and the appropriate touches that ensure possession.

Solving Playing Problems

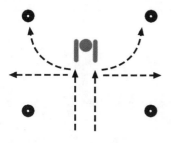

The Four-Cone Placement - The four-cone placement enables the player to work out his best playing options. The way the player moves his body and the number of touch options makes all the difference in being comfortable on the ball in any playing scenario. The best way to develop confidence is to practice in game-like situations. A confident player will take a confrontational touch without any hesitation, whereas a player who lacks confidence will go for the safe option. In terms of training on the practice ground, the players should learn to do both. Most players know instinctively not to take a touch that will give the ball away to the nearest opponent and so they will always choose the safe option. However, the safe option is not always the best option, which is the reason for working on both the safe and the more danger-ous confrontational touch options.

When the defender is marking the attacking player (his team has the ball) tightly, the attacking player can use that to his advantage. The four-cone placement shows SP playing the ball to the player's left foot. In the above example, the player has several options:

1 - He can 'ROLL' the ball around the corner (past the defender) by using the outside of the left foot.
2 - He play the ball with the inside instep of the right foot and move the ball across his own body, thus shielding the ball from the defender.
3 - He can play the forward touch and open up other playing options in that way.

Note - The skill of rolling the ball past the defender is dependent on the player's ability to hold the defender in place physically and to turn on the defender's body position. The roll touch is used in conjunction with the spin around the body of the defender.

Open Up 'The Playing Options'

In higher standards of play it should not matter whether the opponents are behind, in front of or to the side of player A's position. The successful player will know that the success of his action will depend on his ability to control the physical movements that enable him to keep control of the ball. In the following examples, the cone placements to the major directional escape routes enable the player to work on and develop the correct movement attributes to keep possession of the ball against any confrontational defensive posture. The main structure of the working format is again based on the 'Four Cone Placement' and the position of the practicing player in relation to that format. The cones to the outside of the four-cone placement represent the first and second challenger's position.

Learning to Play 'Off' the First Touch

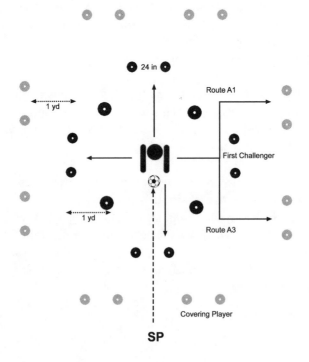

126

Taking On The Challengers - The ability to move with the ball 'off' the first touch involves the practice of moving against the first challenger (against the small black cones) and the covering players to the right or left of the first challenger (against the small grey cones). There are ways of moving the ball that are effective in this respect and there are ways of moving the ball that are ineffective (slow). The above format shows exactly what I mean by that. Some movements are very difficult to perform. It is difficult to move the ball physically to some playing angles. The difficult areas of contention should be highlighted for the player in a practical manner because if he is not aware of the difficulties he will lose possession of the ball. The effect of a wrong touch to a correct playing option will also make a difference between moving correctly with the ball and playing effectively. Why and how this is the case can be experienced in the above working format in a practical way. Work the ball to the guidelines given and experience that for yourself.

Study - Take a look at the red angled cone placements to the side of the blue cones on the outside of the four cone placement (in any direction). I can assure you that these cone placements do reflect the problems of keeping possession against real opponents on the soccer pitch. Taking on the defender successfully depends on the choice of action taken and the physical ability to carry out the movements successfully. The above format enables the player to practice the following considerations -

Safety First - Playing the way you are facing -

In the above example, player A would take the forward touch off the service player in order to play the way he is facing.

Confrontational - Turning back

Man on - It is still possible to turn with the ball when the opponent is placed behind the player receiving the ball. When working in the above format on this problem the first touch is played across the body (right or left). The first cone placements to the outside simulate the position of any second challenger and, therefore, the area where the player takes the next evasive action. Route A1 shows the following escape action sequence: SP passes the ball to player A's right foot; Player A moves the ball across his body to the left on the first touch and on the second touch moves the ball with the inside instep of the right foot to direction A1.

Without Opponents - Moving infield - Play the inside instep 'Extended foot touch' and turn to the left as shown (to escape route A1). This escape route can show you exactly the implications of taking the wrong touch in relation to the escape route. If the player had taken the ball across his body to route A1 (now free of opponents), he would have made the job at hand more difficult than need be. The best way to work the ball to route A1 is to use the foot closest to the escape angle. Taking the extended touch at this point makes it easier to apply the second touch with the inside instep of the right foot because that movement allows for a more natural transition to a 'square on position' off the first touch.

Playing 'Off' 'The Square On' Body Position - The most effective way of playing off the first touch requires the player to master the first touch in such a way that the body is 'Square on' to the next working sequence. Obviously, taking the correct length of touch on the ball is crucial here. If the first touch is too short, the ball will be unplayable and this gives the defender time to affect possession. On other hand, if the touch is too strong the ball will be given away anyway. The same is also true if the player does not move on the touch. Simply stated, in every respect the player's success or failure depends on his ability to move correctly with the ball. For one thing, if the player plays from a square on body position it is very difficult for the opponent to predict the line of attack. For another, it is very difficult to close a player down who can work the ball to the right or left of the defender. The following diagram is a highlighted version of what takes place to the outside of the four-cone placement.

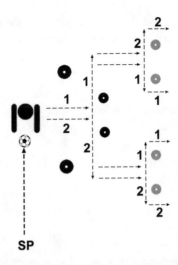

SP

Developing 'The Square on' body position 'off the first touch' -
The breakdown of the format can be seen in this explanation of a
route sequence. The first thing to understand is that it is possible to
break up the format into one working side and position the player in
any format to face the service of the ball from any angle. The main
angle reference points of the service of the ball were shown earlier. In
the above example - Player A takes up the ball facing the SP.

The above represents the outside section of the format. The importance of the square on body position is vital to the player's ability to
move the ball to the left or right of the second cone placement (to the
left or right of the first or second defender). No matter what the reference point is, the same rules apply.

Once the player is 'Square on' to the action.
On taking the first touch and positioning the body 'square on' to the
action, player A practices moving the ball off the line using the skill
options given. This is the view from the air - looking at the player's
actions and movements with the ball. The above diagram shows the
directions of the skill of moving the ball off the line by applying the
inside instep to the ball and the extended touch option - The arrows
represent:

Arrow 1 = The Extended left inside instep position (LF) = Escape route 1
Arrow 2 = The Inside instep of the right foot (RF) across the body = Escape
route 2
In the above format the player learns to move the ball off the line to

the inside and outside of the defender's position, see routes 1 & 2 for examples of that possibility. The idea behind this body position is for the player to be able to read not only the position of the defending players but to also translate the defensive positions into the appropriate action. In practice terms this is made possible by the position of the additional cone placements to the left (in this example) of the player. The above starting position enables the player to -

1 - Practice getting into the square on position 'off the first touch'
2 - Practice looking up off the first touch
3 - Practice assessing the position of the defensive position/s
4 - Working on the physical and technical movements of taking the opponent/s inside/outside

Note - All formats are designed in a way that condenses any playing action scenario into a practical practice format. The service and the position of the working player in relation to the service of the ball also reflects on the need to practice receiving the ball from the appropriate angles of play. In this configuration, SP could play the ball to the practicing player from any realistic distance and angle shown. In this example, the practicing player is receiving the ball from a central defensive position, see diagram.

Playing Attributes - Some people like the look of the attacking 'Wing - backs' as a way of playing soccer. Unfortunately, the development of the player to be able to play the wing back system under the conventional umbrella of training is doubtful. Why? The answer to that is simple - The wing back role requires the player to possess a wide range of playing options such as: the ability to interact with other players, to cross the ball, to finish, to take opponents on, inside or on the outside, running skills/stamina and so on. It is a completely different role to that of the out and out defender or even the conventional winger. In addition to the technical differences, the wing - back's role also requires defensive qualities as well. It is simply impossible to create such a player with conventional back and forward movement based training methods. I believe that the development of such a player can only take place in an open working environment that employs the lateral working formats as part of its training repertoire.

The Playing System

I don't believe that the solution to playing standards comes from the system of play or the player's natural talent, although it is the quality of the player that makes the system effective and not the other way around. The wing back role is a demanding role that cannot be filled by just anyone. I say it

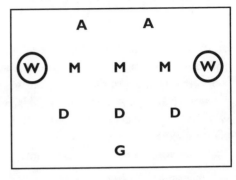

again, it is not the system that wins games but the quality of the player. Some of these contentions make all the difference to the way people approach the development of a player. If you accept that the most important part of any playing system is the player and the skills he contributes to the working system then it is logical from a coaching point of view to implement exercises that reflect on the needs of the player. In other words, the above system of play could not work if the wing - backs did not have the right attributes to make the system work. This is obvious when you consider the new role of the wing - backs. Even excluding the skills factor you can plainly see that the role of the 'Wing Backs' demands greater input from the player on both the attacking and defensive side of the game. The implications, therefore, of what I am saying is quite simple. The wing - back's role cannot be catered to by training methods that develop the 'out and out' defender. The development of such a player needs to focus on the practice of a much wider range of playing options, like for example, his ability to go past defenders, his ability to cross the ball, his ability to interact with midfield players and his ability to defend.

Interactive Training formats - In all respects, part of the training equation has to involve the development of the player's interactive abilities, meaning his ability to play with other players. In an interactive training exercise there are no hiding places. If the player has faults they will be brought to the surface and the player will have to deal with them. Gone are the days where the value of the player is a bag of chips and a bottle of cola - Coaches today cannot ignore the weak areas of a player's game. Higher standards of play depend on the player improving his all round attributes, all of the time. That means working in training environments that will target weaknesses as well as strengths. Here is an example to illustrate my point -

Turning & Hitting Targets - The raising of playing standards depends on many things on both the physical and technical side of the playing equation. It is not just a question of practice, it is also about using working formats and solutions that will develop the player correctly in relation to the playing standards. This requires the player to work in a way that will pay attention to details. Gone are the days where the player makes a hash of things and the 'Coach' turns around and says, 'Bad luck son, better luck next time'.

A TEAM PLAYER - The development of playing standards comes from improving the player's ability to interact with other players correctly. In that context of thinking, here is an example of a working format that helps the player to achieve that objective. In this format the player will practice his ability to play the ball to the correct target with quality in mind and to move correctly in relation to the different options. In this respect there are two important technical considerations here -

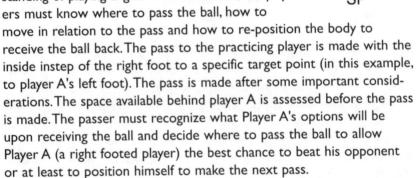

1 - The Quality Of The Pass - To feet - To Space
2 - The Amount Of Touches Taken - Time taken to play

Playing 'OFF' The Reverse Touch - The above pass considerations involve the use and understanding of playing angles. In other words, the players must know where to pass the ball, how to move in relation to the pass and how to re-position the body to receive the ball back. The pass to the practicing player is made with the inside instep of the right foot to a specific target point (in this example, to player A's left foot). The pass is made after some important considerations. The space available behind player A is assessed before the pass is made. The passer must recognize what Player A's options will be upon receiving the ball and decide where to pass the ball to allow Player A (a right footed player) the best chance to beat his opponent or at least to position himself to make the next pass.

Reading the game plan - There are several other things SP has to consider before making the pass to player A. In the above example it is player SP who holds the first key to this interactive playing situation. As we said, SP should assess the playing situation behind player A and decide on the best pass to accommodate a right footed player. In the above example the solution for SP is to play the ball to the left foot of player A (option 2). Why? When player A takes up the pass from SP on the inside instep of his left foot, he will be able to turn and touch the ball onto his stronger right foot. In other words, the ball will be in an excellent position for player A to play his next play option. The pass to the left foot initially by player SP makes it possible for the right - footed player to turn without any problems and to play the next pass straight away with his right foot. Understanding and implementing these considerations will raise the standards of play. The complete action, from the initial pass from SP to the left foot of player A to the pass played by player A to B took just three touches of the ball.

Once player A has turned and is in a position to pass the ball on he will also have to determine the best pass option for returning the ball to Player B.

Interactive Movements 'Off' The Ball

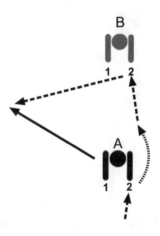

- Passing the ball to the correct foot of player B can make a difference in terms of increasing the playing options. Even if player B is a right - footed player it is sometimes best to make the pass to his left foot. In the above example, the pass is made to player B's left foot in order to make it possible for him to return the pass to player A. Keep in mind that the correct interactive play will demand that player A moves off the pass in support of the pass to player B. A pass to the right foot would reduce the playing options and the playing area. The pass to player B's left foot, on the other hand, opens up an interactive playing solution. When player A passes the ball to player B he invokes the following playing possibilities:

1 - The pass enables player A to move physically to the correct side of player B
2 - This move opens up the possibility of a return pass by player B to player A.
3 - This move makes it easy for player B to pass the ball to his right with his left foot.

4 - The pass by player A leaves player B in a good position to see things in front of player A

5- This pass and move makes it easy for player B to change his playing options.

6 - The angles opened up with this pass helps the technique side of the passing equation.

High standards of play require the player to possess the ability to play the ball with the right and left foot to the above working considerations. Remember that what takes place on the left of the interactive player should also take place on the right. The players quite simply must learn to play the ball to and from either foot if they want to reach a high standard of play.

Developing Economical Movements - Finishing On The Right & Left Foot

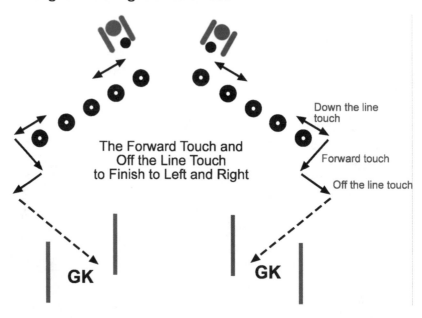

Finishing - During the game a striker may only get one good scoring chance. That chance may well fall on the player's right or left foot. It is not a good idea to get into the habit of re-positioning the body to the ball in order to play the finish with the favorite foot.

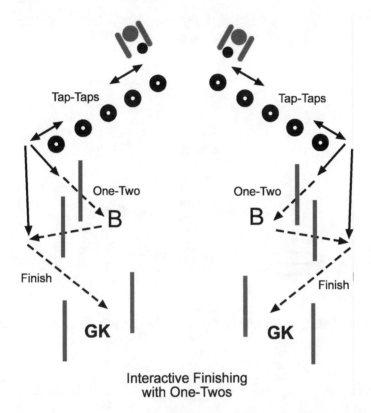

Tap-Taps

Tap-Taps

One-Two

One-Two

B

B

Finish

Finish

GK

GK

Interactive Finishing
with One-Twos

Finishing On The Left And Right Foot - There are different ways to practice finishing. In one-two playing scenarios it is important where the second pass is played. In the above example, the player will not have to take a touch to set the ball up for a strike on target because the finishing set up is actually created by the passing player (player B) who sets the ball up off of a one-two combination.

The Ability To Change Skills In Mid Flow - Improvisation - The ability to change from one skill to another, to use the right and left foot in quick succession or to swap feet in mid flow of a playing sequence, is vital in achieving a high standard of play. In the following example I have a working format that aspires to this objective. Again, we have a working code that the players are able to remember in terms of what the function of each cone placement means, players simply remember the working shapes and translate those into the appropriate physical and therefore technical playing action.

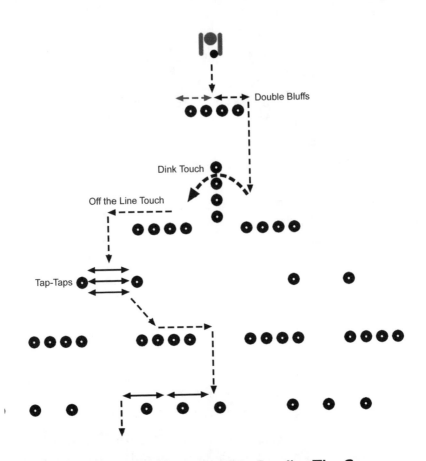

THE CODED WORKING FORMAT - Reading The Cone

Placements In the above 'Maze example', the first touch by player A takes the ball forward with the left or right inside instep. The first line of cones facing player A informs the player to move the ball off the line. The second set of cones informs him to 'dink' the ball over the cones to his right/left. The third set of cones informs player A to move the ball on with the outside of his left foot. Reading the cones and translating the message into actions as the player goes down the format is the name of the game here.

It should be obvious here that the cone placements can be read by the player and translated into the appropriate skill actions. In addition to the above reference points this format is also very useful for developing the player's ability to think on his feet, so to speak. The process of thinking is improved here by the fact that the player has to interpret the cone placements quickly as he moves through the format and apply the correct skill solution to move the ball correctly against a given cone placement position. Each cone placement enables the player to practice his 1v1 skills.

INTERPRETING THE CONE FORMAT
A Two Skill Working format - 'Move the ball off the line & 'Inverted Steps'

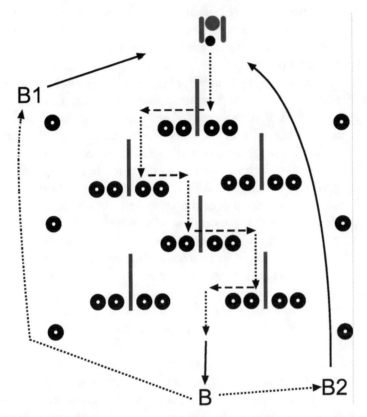

The Working Principles - The main theme of the practice enables the player to practice moving the ball off the line using the 'inverted steps' action. In the overall effort though, allow the player to practice working on alternative movement options as well or a combination of movements that include the use of moving the ball off the line with the outside of the boot. Therefore, in movement option terms the player can work the ball off the line by utilizing such skill actions as the sweep in conjunction with the outside of the boot and the forward touch. To end the sequence, player B (B1) can run back with the ball to the starting position or he can turn and play a long ball (B2) to the next man in.

THE WONDERS OF SCIENCE

When a top is spun - It is the speed of the rotation of the spinning that overcomes the pull of gravity. When this spinning top is travelling fast enough, there exists a 'Balance Moment' in the action where gravity has no influence over the rotation.

The Implications? - Surprisingly, there are quite a lot of implications to the game of soccer that come from this gravity observation. Human beings rely on gravity to stay on earth. However, in terms of the physical ability to move on the ground, the gravity factor is not a friend in every respect of our lives (namely, sport). We need strength to move against gravity and the lateral formats are designed to supply that strength. Let us first of all get back to the 'spinning top'. If it slows down to below a certain spinning ratio, gravity comes into effect and the top falls on its side. You might say, "What has all of this got to do with 'Soccer' training?". The important thing to me in the top's relationship with gravity is the point at which the top falls down. I call this the neutral point between the pull of the earth and the weight of the spinning top. We all live with gravity pulling us down to earth and making some things difficult to do efficiently. In terms of sporting activities we rely on our natural strength to overcome the body weight to gravity ratio to move our body. It is difficult to move the body forward at the best of times, let alone move quickly in anything we do in life. I have, through the development of the working formats, been able to develop a method of training that helps the player to reach a kind of gravitational neutral zone. The physical endeavors in the following 'lateral format' enable the player to develop the strength to stay in that neutral zone. Being quick physically depends on the natural development of the physical side of the player and not on any artificial means. In terms of overall energy development, it is the practice in the lateral movements to the special soccer formations you are about to see that ensures the correct natural physical development.

An Anti-Gravitational Format?

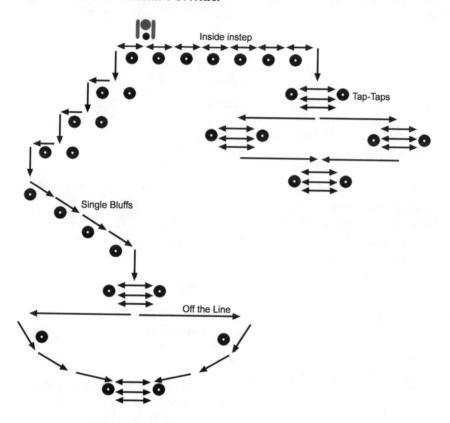

The Combination Format - Linking up the formats creates the correct effect for developing the player's natural strength. This is probably the nearest we can come to a natural anti-gravitational training device. The development of the skills and strength comes from the way the player moves with the ball. This is a very effective working method because the player has to sustain a consistent physical effort of moving the ball to a specific pattern and sequence of skills for a set period of time. In terms of the correct physical effects it is vital to have the correct length of touch in practice because it is the length of touch ('Moving the ball from one inside instep to the other') that generates the necessary 'kinetic tension' for developing natural strength. The anti-gravitational points in the format are the 'fast feet' tap taps and the 'off the line' movements.

Fighting Gravity - If the cone placements are reduced to a fraction of any working format, the pace of the action can be very fast indeed, depending of course on the player's development stage or his ability. Here are some examples of how to develop the art of getting away quickly with the ball 'off' a working skill sequence.

The Skill Of 'Moving 'off' with the ball'

The Simple Shoulder Width Cone Placement - Fast feet action - In this format, the cones are shoulder width apart and player A practices getting away in a forward direction by first dragging the ball back and using a side to forward movement combination.

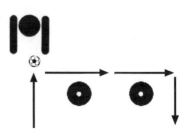

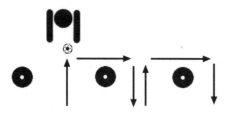

The Three-Cone Fragment

In the three-cone fragment, the sequence involves the player's imaginative use of the ball to any pattern he wishes. The sequence could be - (a) - Drag back (b) - move the ball with the inside instep (c) - Punch the ball forward through the line (d) - Drag the ball back with the underside of the boot (e) - move the ball to the side and explode away forward of the cone placement.

Fighting Gravity

**The Fastest Feet
Format Combination**

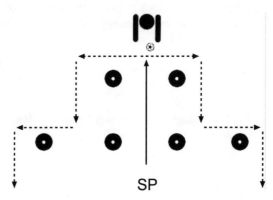

SP

The Inverted Steps

A fragmented format changes the theme of the practice. In the longer formats, the player works on developing the strength for performing the skills in question, whereas in the shorter formats the player works on developing his get away objectives using fast feet movements. 'The shorter the cone placement, the quicker the action'. The development of fast getaways from a tight man on situation can be utilized to turn on the defender or to move away from the defender to any direction. These options are based on the short 'get away' touches. The best way to develop the fast get away is to practice getting away from a standing start. The reason for that is physically motivated. It is simply more difficult to move the ball from a standing start and doing so enhances the ability to get away quickly from any disposition and develops faster touch movements. In the reality of the game such movements can and often are performed when the player is caught in possession of the ball and has to work his way out of a sticky moment. Utilize the drag back, the inside instep, the double bluff, the sweep and inside instep to work out get away combination. Always try to end a fast feet sequence by moving forward away with the ball.

Fast Body Movements - Fast feet are essential to different playing solutions, but so is the ability to move the whole of the body quickly. One of the best ways to develop body speed is to work out in a finishing format. The finishing format is the right working environment in terms of the mental side of the job at hand. The correct effects come from the fact that there are three important playing elements that go towards a good finish.

(a) When the ball comes to the finishing player (A) he needs to possess the ability to make things happen. Essentially that means having the ability to open up space in spite of the defender's presence.

(b) In the modern game the player needs to be able to finish with the right or left foot.

(c) Finish explosively - Possessing Courage - Being first to the ball at times requires courage and mental toughness, this makes up the third element.

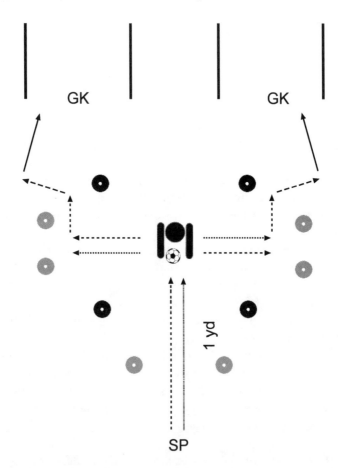

Body Movements - Finishing - Playing off the first touch
The static position of the practicing player is not in any way damaging to the ability of the player to play the ball to different angles nor does it restrict him from possessing the ability to receive the ball from different playing options or angles or from playing the ball to any angle.

The position is representative of a good starting point for developing all the right attributes (physical and technical) for any playing option, including defensive and finishing options. The position of the player and his endeavors to the angles shown develops his abilities to perform the skills in question to a high level of competency. In the above format, player A receives the ball from a service player and works on developing the movements shown by the arrows. Player A moves the ball on the first touch to the guidelines shown for correct effect and thus works the ball to a good position for a finish/strike on goal.

Finishing - Forward Movements Facing The Keeper

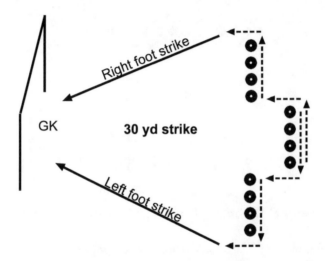

Finishing - One of the most difficult ways to finish is on the forward run with the ball. It is simply harder to strike the ball with pace when the ball is moving away from the player. The best way to overcome this problem is to practice playing the ball forward against the first challenger and the covering player. Both are simulated by the above cone placements. To make the practice simple, the ball is thrown to player A by the goalkeeper. Player A plays against the defending positions to finish.

Note - In terms of the striking distance between the format and the goal, this depends on the age of the players. I would not expect my nine year olds to finish with 30 yd strikes on goal. It is the job of the coach to think in logical terms. The distance from the cone placement to the goals should be set to a logical length depending on the age of the players.

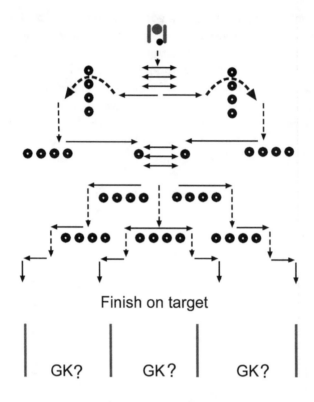

Finish on target

GK?   GK?   GK?

The 'Maradona' Dribbling Run - The Working Format

In this example, the 'Maradona' dribbling run with the ball ends with a strike on one of the three goals. You can have one goalkeeper move between the goals to condition the game. Tell the players to finish where the keeper is to force them to look up prior to striking the ball.

THE CREATION OF A NEW SKILL - To stimulate the player's ability to create 'New' ways of moving the ball, keep changing the working shape to create different problems. When linked to the player's existing abilities, the following format can also help to develop the ability to form new close ball control skill combinations.

The Mixed Training Format

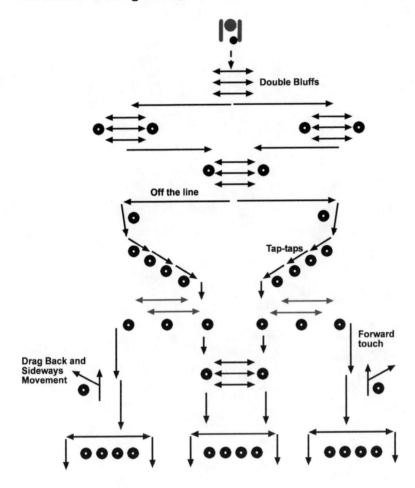

Double Bluffs

Off the line

Tap-taps

Forward touch

Drag Back and Sideways Movement

THE CRAFT OF PASSING

You can have all the on-the-ball skills in the world but if you can't pass the ball for toffee it's all a waste of time. The good news is that the skill of passing the ball is not as difficult to teach as you might imagine. As in all skill options the pass has certain characteristics that you can work with to improve this ability. The following passing formats are designed to bring out the correct physical and technical movements naturally that make the pass efficient and correct from every aspect of play. There are obviously principles here that the player will have to keep to if he is to master the art of passing the ball. These principles of passing are as follows -

(a) Look up and assess
(b) Keep your eye on the ball
(c) Look down and control the ball (excepting one touch play)
(d) Play the ball with the correct foot/position/skill

The above sequence (a) to (d) needs further explanation. Suffice to say that there are different problems associated with making the pass. The main faults come from the player's inability to distinguish between the different ways of passing the ball.

(a) The 'laces' - playing the long ball

(b) The inside instep - playing the short pass

Most passing skills have one of the above foot positional requirements or a mixture of both where the ball is played by neither the full laces nor the full inside instep but something in - between. When playing the long ball the foot position is shown as position (a) = The laces part of the boot to the ball. When playing the short pass the foot position is shown as (b) = The inside instep to the ball. In practical terms there are a number of problems therefore, that can arise from different sources that affect the quality of the pass such as, for example, the size of the player's foot, the age of the player and his strength factor. Such factors can play a part in making it difficult to pass the ball effectively.

Note - When it comes to the younger players do not introduce a smaller ball into the working equation. There are lots of technical reasons for using a ball that has the full working dimensions of the real game of soccer. The lifting of the foot is an important technical habit that has an effect on any number of playing options. The development of the player must include the ability to perform a wide range of lateral and forward to back movements with the ball by lifting their foot to the proper height of touch, length of touch and roll of the ball. The roll of the ball and the height of the ball plays a crucial part in that development process. A lighter ball is fine, but keep to the big ball in terms of size because of the developmental foot to ball implications.

The Inside Instep Pass Format

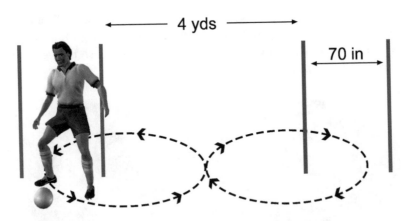

The Stage By Stage Approach - Allow me to take you the long way round to explain the above simple but effective format on the development of the ability to play the ball with the inside instep of the right and left foot. There are important working principles that you must work on if you are to improve the ability of the player to pass the ball. It does matter whether the pass is made over a distance of ten yards or thirty yards. Here are the most important working progressive principles.

Stage 1 - The habit of moving to the ball rather than waiting for the ball to come to you is the first working principle of the above exercise and in any session on the development of the ability to pass the ball. Keep in mind that the ability to pass the ball is also linked to the ability to receive the ball. My work on this issue begins with a simple exercise that instils the 'move to the ball' habit.

Move out of the gate

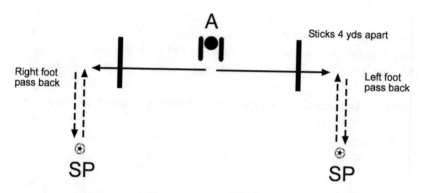

Getting The Body Behind The Ball - Move out - Pass & Move - The practicing player is positioned between the two sticks as shown and keeps face on to the SPs. The gap between the two sticks is about 4 ft. The pass from the SPs is performed to coincide with player A's movements out of the center of the two sticks. Naturally, player A knocks the ball back to SP1 or SP2 every time he moves out to the side, keeping 'Square on' when doing so. The above working sequence shows the pass back to SP from the right and or left side of the sticks.

In Practice - The sequence, therefore, is as follows; Player A moves back (out) and sideways to his left - the pass comes in from SP - player A plays the ball back to SP with the inside instep of the left foot, moves 'off that pass' back to in-between the sticks, fast feet in the sticks on the spot and moves out quickly, timing his move out to coincide with what SP is doing. Player A moves out to get behind the ball and knocks the ball back with the inside instep of the right foot, this time to SP's right foot and so on.

So, Player A passes the ball - right foot to SP's right foot, left foot to SP's left foot. SP on other hand plays in the following sequence - Right foot controls the ball, left foot plays the ball (left foot to left foot), Left foot controls the ball, right foot plays the ball (right foot to right foot). The above movements can only take place if there is cooperation between SP and the practicing player. SP keeps the practice going by making sure that he times his pass to coincide with player A's movements in the format.

Passing The Ball On The Move - Once the skill of getting behind the ball is understood, move on to work on the simple understanding of how the body works in relation to supporting the pass and the physical technique of playing the ball. The fundamental touch options will be the 'Inside instep' and the 'laces' techniques to the ball. The upright body position lends itself to playing the ball with the 'Inside instep' and the 'lean to' body position lends itself to playing the ball with the laces.

General Instructions - Lean to - Working with the 'Laces to the ball' If the format is on 'The laces to the ball' then you require 2 SPs and 1 ball. On the other hand, if the format is on the inside instep to the ball only, you will require two SPs and 2 balls.

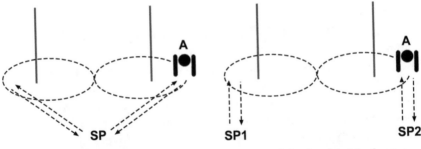

Pass with the Laces   **Pass with the Inside Instep**

This is because the pass made with the laces part of the boot will be played back diagonally across to any service player - and the pass back from the inside instep will be played forward of the working player directly to the SP. The service of the ball to the player on both counts coincides with his figure eight running pattern (see figure eight run and SP target options for more details). There are of course any number of technical problems for the passing player to work out, here are some of the major contenders -

**Negative Spin & Shaping Up To Take The Pass - ** The simple pass can be affected by a lack of understanding as to the role of the body in playing the pass. The ability to use the body properly to take up the ball or to make the pass comes from an understanding of how to acquire the following attributes.

(a) The ability to shape the body to receive the ball
(b) The ability to shape the body to make the pass

**The practical translation - ** It is important to use the body properly to receive and pass the ball. The incorrect body shape or foot position to the ball can impart spin on the ball or even make the pass inaccurate.

**The Quality Of The Pass - ** You would be surprised at how important some of the above - mentioned technical aspects of passing are to the quality of the pass. Taking the spin out of the ball amounts to better ball control situations and more accuracy in the pass mainly because when the ball is played without spin it is usually because the player has made the pass with a good follow through and with the correct foot position to the ball.

**Accuracy - ** The quality of the pass is also greatly helped by the correct positioning of the body.

By positioning the body correctly in terms of passing the ball it is relatively easy to take the negative spin (bad for ball control) out of the working equation. Negative spin comes about because the player passing the ball did not position himself correctly in relation to the receiving player. The safest body position for a return pass is always to face the same direction as the recipient of the pass. The accuracy of the pass on the move can be helped by -

1 - Taking the foot to the ball that is furthest away from the receiving player
2 - Making the pass with the flush part of the inside instep of the foot

The position of the body makes a difference to the pass. So does the use of the correct foot to the ball. In this next example we can see how easy it is to work on shaping the body to the pass and on taking the correct foot and technique to the ball.

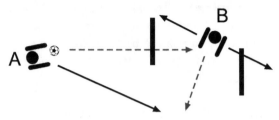

Shape up - You don't need elaborate training routines to practice all the working principles of the pass. The 'two stick' 'One-Two' example above will do the job nicely. The players simply work a one-two past the sticks in a back and forward fashion. -

Explanation of the working format - When player A passes the ball to player B, he does so with the laces of his left boot to the ball. The pass is made to player B's left foot. Player B shapes up to face the pass from player A and plays the ball back to player A between the sticks with the inside instep of his left foot, aiming the ball to the space in front of the runner (player A). Just two passes into the working format and I have already implemented two of the more important passing principles - how to 'shape up' to receive the ball and where to play the ball.

Next

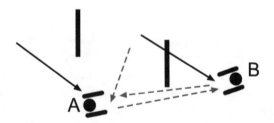

Next - Player B needs to go past the stick facing him after playing the ball to player A. Player B turns at the point you see and shapes up to play the pass from player A with the laces part of his left boot back to player A. Player A turns 'off' the pass to player B and shapes up to go back in the direction of the starting position. B plays the ball in front of player A and so on - All of this is done in quick succession. The sequence centers on the practice of shaping up to take the ball/pass the ball back.

The working principles of the above format - The ability to move on the touch makes the ball exchanges between players A and B work. The accuracy of the pass depends on it and so does being in the right place at the right time. In simple terms, if the body position in relation to the pass is incorrect then I can assure you that both players will end up chasing the ball. The explanation of the skills involved ends when player B knocks the ball back diagonally to the left foot (top side of the format) (to player A). At that point the whole sequence can be repeated as many times as you wish. The one-two sequence can be changed to add a long pass option to this practice format sequence, for example

The Short and Long Pass Option Format

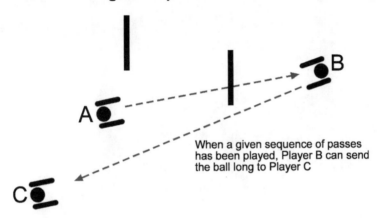

When a given sequence of passes has been played, Player B can send the ball long to Player C

The Practice Of The Long Pass - A Rotational Format - When you wish to add the long pass into the practice equation, simply position a third player as shown to the outside of the format. When both players have moved the ball to a set number of one-twos past the sticks, allow one player to knock the long ball to player C as shown in this example. The long pass is then supported by the player who played the pass (player B) - The receiving player plays another one-two with the now supporting player B. The final pass in this sequence by B plays player C in to move up to the format with the ball to take his turn in the sticks. The players rotate off the long pass option.

Developing Confidence and The Thinking Process

Gaining Confidence - It is not easy for any young player to assert his physical presence on the soccer pitch. Some players may feel that by 'Shouting' out loud they may offend their teammates. Others may lack the confidence to do so simply because they are naturally shy. Whatever the problem, there are natural methods of training that will overcome such mental problems. Young or old, players need help with the mental side of the game and it is possible to provide that help without compromising the players or leaving them to fend for themselves. Simple body language forms are not difficult to comprehend or learn and in fact this 'silent' form of communication on the pitch is often all that is needed to convey individual playing intentions. Knowing something about what could happen next on the soccer pitch can save some players their nervous energy and give them confidence.

Simple Body Language

Hand raised in the air -

"I am looking to play the long ball"

Hands lower by the side -

"I am looking for someone to come short"

When I am not looking at you -

"I don't want the ball"

When I am looking at you -

"I want the ball"

I am running -

"I want someone to come and help me keep possession"

I am turning -

"I will need help to keep possession. Come short to me "

The Not So Obvious - Saving Nervous Energy - Above are very simple body language cues that help the players to save nervous energy but it should also be obvious by now that the development of the correct way of moving and playing will also save the player nervous (and therefore physical) energy. There is another way to save lots of energy that may not be so obvious. If the training sessions are simple and the players understand what is required straight away, this will also save them nervous energy. The use of visual formats that are easy to learn costs less effort and in turn saves energy. Action does speak louder than words and working rather than talking is the best way to teach anyone. Here are further examples of that -

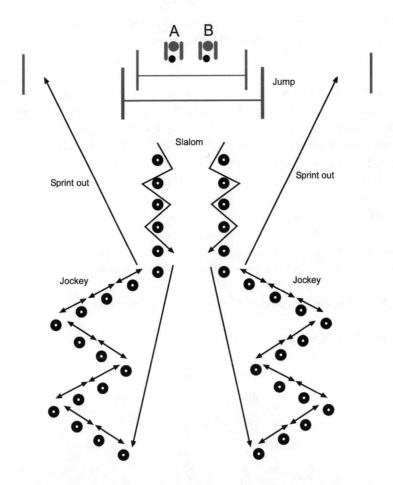

WOW ! What confusion! Not really, it may look complicated but I can assure you I have nine year olds that go through this format with their eyes closed (well, almost). Obviously, if you are working with younger players you don't want to have too many elements in the same format. However, it is quite surprising just how well nine year olds can cope with this type of work without any stress. In truth you can govern the nature and duration of the effort by applying restrictions on time or the number of runs made. In a mixed group of players I have found it quite easy to say to the younger lads to make one run to every three runs made by the older players. If the player knows exactly what is required of him, he will be less stressed.

Mental & Physical Reaction Training

The development of the physical side of the player goes hand in hand with his mental development. For example, 'The Players Attitude' and his 'Confidence' in different problem situations on the soccer pitch. There are different natural ways of working on the mental state of the player. One of the best methods of training for developing 'Confidence' involves teaching the player to react more quickly to any given playing situation on the soccer pitch. Obviously if a player reacts late to a loose ball often enough, his confidence will suffer. Late reactions will also have consequences in other areas, such as the spending of energy as the player must constantly 'chase' the game. I have already pointed out that there are different fitness forms in soccer that you need to work with in order to develop the player's physical and mental capabilities. Quick reactions will obviously afford the player more time on the ball. It is logical to conclude, therefore, that if the player has better playing solutions he will be better able to conserve energy.

The 'Thinking Process' Development Formats

THE CIRCLE

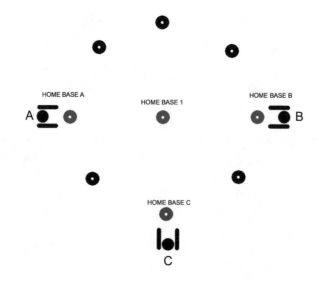

Simple But Effective - You may be surprised to learn that you don't need elaborate instructions to have the proper effect on your players' thinking process. In fact, the simpler formats are the best because it is not the instructions but the overall concept that is most important. The circle can be utilized as a warm up exercise in this thinking development process. In the 'circle format' the players are allocated a home base and the instructions from the 'Coach' are interpreted by the players into appropriate movements. For example: if 'Coach' says "Home base 1", the players sprint to the center cone and back to their home base cone; if 'Coach' says "Home base", all the players run around the circle on the outside (clockwise or counterclockwise) and back to their home base blue cone. 'Coach' follows this up by calling out the next instructions.

Expanding the thought process - To the above humble beginning we now add more physical requests to the simple home base and home base 1 options - Example - Jog two cones to the right (up two cone placements) - jog one back (back one cone placement). It is simple to make up a working movement sequence from this basic concept. We then add other instructions such as - Sideways straddle two cone placements, jog one cone placement, home base (players run around the circle clockwise to home base) and so on, its that simple - What makes it work is the fact that no matter how simple the instructions are, the players will still need to interpret the instruction into the correct physical actions. I have found that it is quite easy to put pressure on the players by changing the instructions often or by simply asking the players to work to a pre - set sequence.

Simple Physical & Mental Pressure
The Sprint & Mix Format

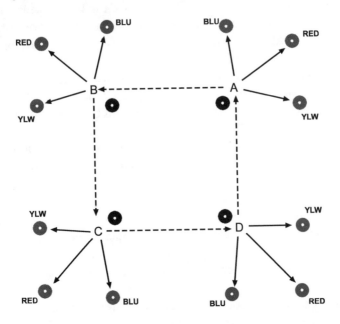

Group Competition - It is difficult for most underdeveloped players to listen to instructions and to carry them out without making any mistakes. The concentration levels of any player can be developed to a higher standard by a method of training that involves the use of a request task sequence. In that method of training the players simply listen to the instructions and translate them into the correct physical actions. The format above is a simple example of this method of training. The sequence instruction possibilities in the above format are as follows - (1) All players run, jog or walk on the outside of the square (2) Jog 'Corner to corner' (3) Jog one corner, sprint to the next (4) Walk around the square (5) Jog, jog, walk, walk, sprint to a color . . . Phew! Is that all? Well that's what you need to do in order to develop the ability to think ahead and the concentration to carry out more than one playing option. Confidence comes from the ability to carry out the instructions without making a mistake.

Piling On The Pressure - It is easy to put more pressure on the players. Simply look for the last man to move correctly and carry out the given instruction. The pressure comes from adding more and more instructions or changing the instructions constantly. The color cones are 'The Sprint Outs' and are represented by the short arrows pointing out to the cone in each of the four corners of the square. 'Coach' barks out the following orders - 'Corner to corner' - 'Stop' (stop at corner and jog in place) - 'Blue' (sprint to blue cone and back to the corner) - 'Red' - 'Corner to corner' - 'Turn' (move in opposite direction) - 'Stop' - 'Green' - and so on. It is up to the 'Coach how much time the players need to spend in each corner of the format.

Think & React - COMPETE

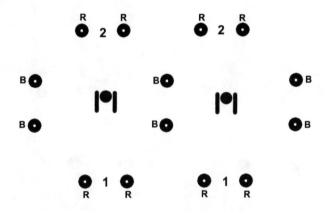

One On One - There are ways to toughen up the players mentally. Here is a one on one competition format that can instill the competitive mentality. Instructions - The above format is a simple gate formation. In this example, we have the red gate 1 in front of each player and red gate 2 behind each player. We also have a left and right side gate to the side of the players. The position of the color - coded gates constitute a working code. In this example, the players react first to a two - color call. The 'Coach' barks out the simple instructions. Who will react first? - For example, 'Red 1! Red 2!' - On hearing this call each player interprets the instructions and sprints through the red gate 1, goes around the outside and back through red gate 2 - The first player to run out through gate 1 and back inside through gate 2 wins.

The Alternative Instruction - You can change the format and make things more difficult for the players by using more than two colors. In that case the call of the 'Coach' could be 'Blue, Yellow, Red, Green' - The translation of this call into action is as follows: Players run out of the blue gate, back in through the yellow gate, out through the red gate and back in through the green gate. It is the players' responsibility to listen and to translate what is said into action. I should point out that being first to translate the command into action correctly is the main objective here.

To further test the players, you can ask them to do the opposite of what you call.

Getting to the Ball - Colors and Numbers

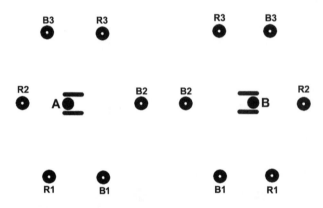

Instructions - In this mental and physical reaction format, players A & B compete against each other to be the first to touch the color cones called. On each call players move to the instruction and back to position A/B. Slightly in front and to the side of players A/B there is a - Blue (on the left) and Red (on the right) cone. Slightly behind and to the side of the players there is a - Blue (to the right) and Red (to the left) cone. Directly behind each player about 1.5 yds away is a Red cone and in front about 1.5 yds away is a Blue cone. Both players react to the call of the 'Coach', who shouts out a color and number (ex. 'Blue 2') and the player who reacts and moves to the correct cone and back to the starting position wins!

Additional Instructions - The players could also be given instructions such as - 'Turn' (turn on the spot) or 'Swap' (swap positions with the other player). Complex combinations can put real pressure on the players: 'Turn, Swap, Red 1' or 'Turn, Turn, Blue 1, Swap, Turn, Red 2' and so on.

The Battling Format - How do you teach the players to be competitive and ensure that no one gets hurt in the process. No one likes the thought of getting hurt in training . The following format is designed for the players to use their hands and body to compete against the competition.

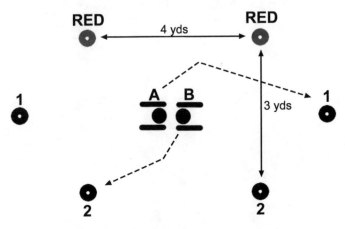

Mental Toughness - The physical side of the game can be introduced to the player in this simple but effective format that is both safe and fun. To achieve the practice of the battling objectives that are required to 'toughen' up the playing mentality, players are positioned 'back to back' in relation to the three cones placed in front of each player. When the 'Coach' calls out a color or a number each player tries to be the first to move to the color/number cone given, not to the cones in front of him but to the cones behind him. Each player will have to do his best to prevent the other player from turning and achieving the given objective. Play to ten.

THE CHOREOGRAPHY TRAINING SESSION

Not too long ago, the typical coaching session was made up of -

1 - Running For Fitness
2 - A Form Of Team Training
3 - Playing Soccer.

I hardly ever saw anyone work on the skills side of the game to any extent. Of course more and more now, things are actually beginning to change somewhat and people everywhere are beginning to realize the value of changing their training sessions to include a wider range of training options. I have over the last fifteen years or so produced a training environment that includes a major input of additional working concepts to the existing methods of training.

The Major Areas of Player Development now possible include -

(a) The Warm Up
(b) Physical Body Coordination - Lateral Movements
(c) Close Ball Control Skills
(d) Moving The Ball Off The Line
(e) The Actual Development Of The First Touch
(f) Playing possession

A to F would in fact be sufficient to the lateral training session objectives, however, in addition to the above considerations there is a need to bring the skills in question into the practical reality of the game of soccer. Therefore, in addition to the above considerations we have the following soccer training concepts that are now included and utilized for the development of the playing side of the working equation -

1 - The Half Field Format
2 - Match Fitness

Some of the above objectives can be found in my first book called 'The Soccer Coaching Handbook' (Reedswain Publishing).

The Make Up of a Modern Training Session.
On completing the 'Warm Up' part of the training session, 'The First Format' is made up of all the elements that I believe a player needs to work with in terms of his physical coordination requirements.

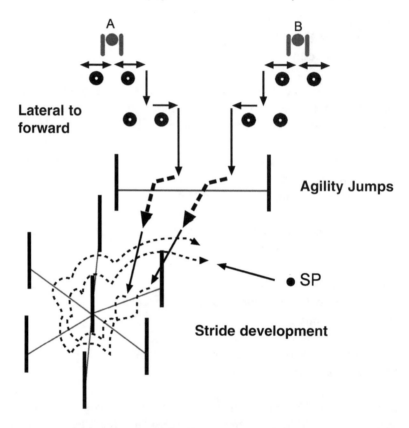

The General Make Up Of The Format - Here we have 'lateral to forward' movements for developing lateral to forward feet co-ordination. This is followed up by the agility jump and then the stride foot coordination movements in the circle.

Note - When working in pairs - The competition here is based on which player manages to be first through the format and carry out a one-two sequence with SP. Up to ten reps per player.

Next comes the work on close ball control skills with the simple introduction of the inside instep work found in the straight line of cones format. At this point in the training session we are interested in the strength side of the equation, so players just need to work on the simple inside instep movements across the straight line of cones format.

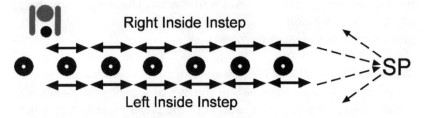

In Practice - The players move the ball down the line with the inside instep of the right and left foot. Remember the balance side of the equation. The players can play a one-two with SP before taking their turn back in the format. Players have a ball each. Duration of the practice is 10 to 15 min.

Practicing the sweep movement - Next, all players will work on developing the movements for the close ball control skill of sweeping the foot over the ball. The height of the tape should be a little higher than the height of the ball. In this format the players concentrate on the physical side of the movement without the ball. The movement sequence, however, can be rounded off by playing a one-two with the service player (who can be positioned with a ball at his feet for that purpose) - before moving back up to the starting position again. Duration of the practice is 10 to 15 minutes.

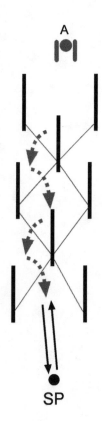

Note - On average a two-hour training session requires up to 8 formats and the time spent on each format could be anything up to approximately 15 minutes per format. However - If you only have 90 minutes, obviously you must select fewer formats, perhaps even as low as 3 would be enough to take care of that time span. Older players won't mind working on a specific skill for a long period of time, but the younger ones will get tired quickly and can get bored with one training routine if it lasts more than fifteen minutes or so. Varied work is the key to making practice fun for young players.

Note - If a training format has been difficult or tiring for the players, give them a ten minute 'break' to run with the ball. This will stretch their legs and get the blood circulating again, and they should be ready to move back into the working format.

Working The Ball Off The Line - Our number 4 format deals with the practice of moving the ball off the line by applying the sweep and other options. The sequence ends with the player sending a long ball to the next man in. We have kept the practice of close ball control in line with the work theme of the second format. We are now ready to move on to the next working topic.

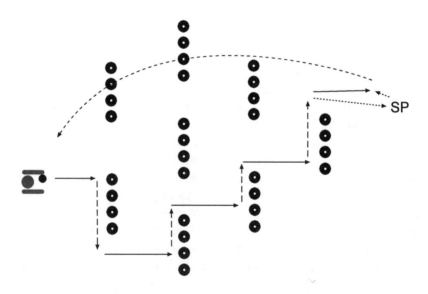

INTERPRETING THE CONE PLACEMENTS

In time, players will be able to 'read' the cone placements and know automatically what skills are involved. Here is a breakdown of the cone placements and their corresponding skill movements:

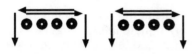 #1 - Moving the ball off the line-right or left - for opening up areas of play or moving against an on-coming opponent

#2 - Dinking the ball over a defender's foot as he lunges in for the ball - lift the ball over the opponent's foot with the left or right foot.

 #3 - Move the ball backwards, sideways and forward. This skill is utilized for moving the ball forward away from an approaching defender.

#4 - Taking on a backpedaling defender by moving the ball to the angle shown and sending the defender the wrong way.

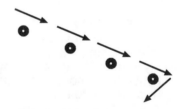

 #5 - **The Drag Back and Inside Instep Sweep.** Taking the ball out of a tight man on situation.

#6 - **Lateral and Forward Touch**
The inside instep of the left foot moves the ball laterally to the right and the right foot makes the forward touch. Used to help the player move past the first challenger and a covering defender.

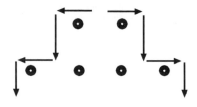

#7 - Playing the ball with the inside instep - right to left foot - left foot to right foot and the Forward Touch at either end. Essential to the development of the strength and technique needed to perform various skills.

#8 - **Tap Taps** - performed with the inside instep of the right and left foot. Puts the player into a position from which he can send the defender the wrong way.

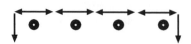

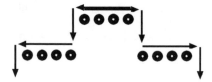

#9 - Moving the ball off the line against a covering player

#10 - **Fast Feet** - Single inside instep movements. **Double Backs** - moving one way then back the other way. Combination movements that are designed to send the opponent the wrong way.

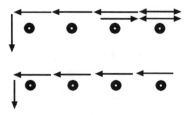

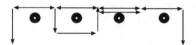

#11 - More Fast Feet movements **Drag Backs, Sweeps, Inside Insteps, Forward Touch**